TEXAS
50 HIKES WITH KIDS

TEXAS
50 HIKES
WITH KIDS

WENDY GORTON
AND NINA PALMO

Timber Press · Portland, Oregon

Frontispiece: Our hiking crew on the Montezuma Quail Trail

Published in 2023 by Timber Press, Inc., a subsidiary of Workman
Publishing Co., Inc., a subsidiary of Hachette Book Group, Inc.

1290 Avenue of the Americas
New York, New York 10104

timberpress.com

Printed in China on responsibly sourced paper

Series design by Hillary Caudle
Cover design and illustration by Always With Honor
All maps by David Deis

The publisher is not responsible for websites (or their content) that are not
owned by the publisher.

The Hachette Speakers Bureau provides a wide range of authors for
speaking events. To find out more, go to HachetteSpeakersBureau.com or
email HachetteSpeakers@hbgusa.com.

ISBN 978-1-64326-161-4

A catalog record for this book is available from the Library of Congress.

To Stacee, for taking a chance and believing in my vision for helping all kids embrace adventure!

To my mother, Ginny, whose practical support is the backbone of all my adventures and whose trust in independence grew the adventurer in me.
—Wendy

To Ralph, my adventure partner forever. To Elsa and Linnea—watching you grow will always be our greatest and most important adventure.
—Nina

CONTENTS

PREFACE

The natural beauty and rich history and culture of Texas pack in enough adventure to last a lifetime. This book provides a kid-friendly introduction to the vast landscape of Nina's adopted home state, from the rugged beauty of West Texas to the sparkling rivers of the Hill Country of Central Texas to the lush forests of the Piney Woods of East Texas. You'll find hikes in each ecoregion of Texas, with the aim of helping children and families gain knowledge of the natural world. Along the way, we hope hikers will reap the benefits that come with outdoor adventure but are too often lost in the race to achieve—resilience, healthy risk-taking, unplugging from technology and hyperconnectivity, and having fun. Each hike in this book has been tested and approved by Nina's kids to ensure we are sharing fun adventures that grow a love of nature and exploration.

Nina's own childhood was filled with outdoor adventures in Finland and Michigan, the two places she spent her growing-up years. From a young age, her parents took her cross-country skiing on the frozen inlets of the Baltic Sea outside their apartment building and ice skating on neighborhood ball fields transformed into outdoor rinks. Summers were spent camping and road-tripping around the United States with extended family, squeezing ten people, four tents, a large cooler, and a backpack apiece into two cars and hitting the road. Although these adventures may paint an idyllic scene, they were also filled with incessant mosquitoes, freezing nights in tents, and fires that wouldn't start in the rain. She learned to weather the unexpected and find satisfaction in facing new challenges head-on.

As an educator and parent, Nina hopes to inspire a new generation to experience the wonder and awe that comes from interacting with the natural beauty of the world around us, along with the character-building life lessons that are inevitably built into outdoor adventures. We believe a

Most Americans can cover their home state in less than a week. In Texas, if you concentrate and work at it steadily, you can traverse your territory by about age thirty-seven.

—Rosemary Kent, author of
Genuine Texas Handbook

major challenge facing our education system is the need to integrate traditional academic learning with physical and mental well-being, and we see experiences in the natural world as crucial to a better future. We hope to spark curiosity and make education come alive. We encourage children to experience the thrill of scientific discovery, explore the languages of nature, and immerse themselves in the beautiful and sometimes terrible stories of the people who walked this land before them. In the words of parent educator and author Pam Leo, we need to understand that kids learn by *asking* questions, not by answering them.

When it comes to education, we can shift our perspective to see the forest, not just the trees. We can zoom out from a narrow focus on reading levels and math facts and ask whether a child is engaged with the world, asking questions, discovering real problems and solutions, being creative, and thinking about others. There is a reason kindergarten was originally conceived as a children's garden. Nature is the perfect setting to engage with the world hands-on and begin gathering the experiences that form the basis for more abstract understandings of math, science, ecology, history, engineering, art, and many other areas of study later in life. It's time to reclaim a model of education that includes sunshine and trees, not just fluorescent lights and desks.

These ideas form part of the underpinnings of Nina's philosophy of Raising Wildflower Kids (you're invited to visit her website, RaisingWildflowerKids.com). It's an approach to family life and education that leaves overscheduling behind and provides plenty of opportunity for free play, imagination, and deep bonds with the ones closest to us. It relies on the knowledge that wildflowers are resilient, but also recognizes the importance of early life and the environment for thriving and growth. It relies on previewing experiences and showing kids what the world has to offer. Nature is a showcase of the amazing feats many different creatures

Two young adventurers climbing rock outcroppings

accomplish in their habitats. Our children are no exception; we sometimes forget that the outdoors is their natural habitat.

We recognize that there are lots of barriers today that prevent families from getting outside into nature. Not everyone has access to green space. Kids and parents are exhausted after a day of school and work. If we do manage to get outside, there may be no other families around, so everyone gets bored quickly. Bring other kids along on adventures. Peter Gray, a Boston College research professor and expert on children's play, explains, "When you go on a hike or a trip, think about inviting other families or joining group hikes. Kids need other kids. This frees you, the adult, as well as your child, so you can interact with other adults. They can go ahead safely on the trail, and you don't have to go and amuse them because they are learning and playing with their peers. Don't try to cover too much ground—stop and let them play wherever they are."

Perhaps the biggest barrier is that we as a culture are led to believe we can do without nature. We are told that the most important priority is to drill academic skills from a young age and then go outside if there is time. Raising Wildflower Kids means flipping the script and recognizing experiences in the natural world as the foundation for learning and skill-building. We won't know what our kids are capable of unless they have a chance to experience what nature offers.

Children need opportunities to move and take risks, to build and create, to touch and to smell, to imagine and to play, to test their limits and build confidence, to unplug from distractions and focus on the here and now, to look at the world around them and wonder.

How can we best design experiences that inspire wonder in our children and provide such opportunities? That is the question to keep in mind as you use this book, too. If we can provide a fun environment and the initial sparks of curiosity, we can—as educators, caregivers, aunties and uncles, grandparents, and parents—help children discover and explore the world around them and learn to appreciate natural beauty even from the youngest age. The aim of this guide is to give adults tools to help ignite questions on the trail, to teach kids that it's great to stop and look at things instead of just rushing from point A to point B, and to introduce a broader understanding of just how many unique places they live near. By simply venturing out and interacting with kids along the trail, we are helping them build the skills they need to learn how to question things they see around them—everywhere—and to look for answers.

Many of these adventures provide a taste of treks kids may embark on as older kids, college students, or adults—imagine them summiting Guadalupe Peak, the highest natural point in Texas, in a few years or tackling the full 128-mile Lone Star Hiking Trail as young adults. In the meantime, this guide aims to provide kids of all ages with a curated selection of some of the most varied and interesting destinations in Texas while reassuring busy adults about what to expect from any given trail, the features they'll see when they arrive, and the logistics that can make or break an outdoor excursion with kids.

The number of "kid-friendly" hikes in Texas is almost staggering, but we developed a firm Kid Filter of awesome features, simple driving, and turnkey instructions on the trail so you're not second-guessing yourselves. You'll get honest-to-goodness dirt under your shoes rather than pavement, giving a more adventurous and genuine hiking experience rather than a sterile stroll. As you romp with your own crew, just keep in mind that while the scavenger hunt items called out on each hike might help you to add excitement or teachable moments, finding all of them shouldn't be the main goal of your outing.

We hope this guide will help you foster curiosity and a love of nature in the kids in your lives. We hope by putting the guidebook in their hands, the next generation of naturalists will be inspired. Experiencing the wonders all around us creates lifelong habits of seeking out adventure, appreciating the gifts nature gives us every day, and caring about keeping our natural resources clean, beautiful, and accessible for many future generations as well.

On a final note, discussions about safety and belonging in the outdoors are difficult but necessary. Although the vast majority of people we have encountered in nature have been friendly, we prefer to hike with friends, especially in remote areas without cell-phone service. We feel a sense of safety in numbers. Unfortunately, this sense of safety is often lacking for outdoor enthusiasts in BIPOC and LGBTQ+ communities. These groups are also more likely to face barriers to outdoor life, including a lack of access to green spaces, financial constraints, and direct or indirect signals that they are not welcome. Here in Texas state and local parks are sometimes named after people who fought against racial equality and civil rights. For example, the namesake of Martin Dies, Jr. State Park in East Texas is a Texas politician who signed the Southern Manifesto, condemning the Supreme Court's 1954 decision to end school segregation. The park was named after him in 1965.

This issue led environmental educator and author James Edward Mills to coin the term "adventure gap" to describe the racial divide in outdoor activities. Addressing this gap is important for many reasons. First and foremost, it's a basic matter of safety and fairness. Everyone deserves to enjoy the benefits of the outdoors without worrying about being a target of violence or harassment. Second, the protection of the natural world depends on it. The beauty of the next generation is that it is more diverse than ever before. This means we have a greater responsibility to make the outdoors welcoming to all. As Mills cautions us, "If nothing happens to change the disparity between those who spend time in nature and those who don't, we'll have a constituency of voters in this country who have little or no relationship with the outdoors."

Our hope is that as we enjoy nature with our children, we'll strive for an outdoors that makes everyone feel welcome.

CHOOSING YOUR ADVENTURE

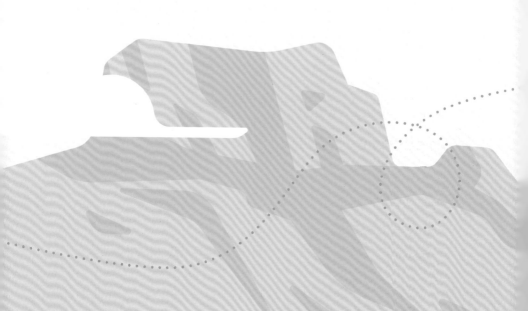

This guide is designed to help your children become co-adventurers with you across the diverse landscape of the Lone Star State, so build excitement by involving them in the planning process from the beginning. Let them flip through and mark the pages they'd like to tackle in the future. Ask them what features they love to encounter when they're outside and what parts of Texas they want to explore. Each entry includes info on the closest town or adventure hub. For maximum success with younger kids, no hike is over 5 miles long or has more than 800 feet in elevation gain—perfectly attainable for most little legs. This means there can be plenty of time for exploration, rest stops, snacks, and just taking in the sights and sounds around you.

ADVENTURES IN WEST TEXAS / BIG BEND COUNTRY

ADVENTURE	HUB	LENGTH (MILES)	DIFFICULTY/ ELEVATION	HIGHLIGHTS
1 Santa Elena Canyon PAGE 62	Terlingua / Marfa / El Paso	1.7	Challenging 148'	Canyon, river, desert flora
2 Lower Burro Mesa Pouroff Trail PAGE 66	Terlingua / Marfa / El Paso	1	Easy 200'	Dry waterfall, desert flora
3 Basin Loop Trail PAGE 70	Terlingua / Marathon / El Paso	1.8	Moderate 289'	Geological views, cool flora and fauna
4 Montezuma Quail Trail PAGE 74	Terlingua / Marfa / El Paso	1.1	Moderate 240'	Geological views, wildlife
5 Chihuahuan Sky Island PAGE 78	Terlingua / Marfa / El Paso	2.3	Challenging 358'	Canyon, scenic views, geological exhibit
6 Smith Spring PAGE 82	El Paso	2.3	Moderate 402'	History, tranquil spring
7 Monahans Sandhills PAGE 86	Midland / Odessa / Marfa	1.3	Easy 16'	Windswept dunes, wildflowers

ADVENTURES IN
THE PANHANDLE PLAINS

ADVENTURE	HUB	LENGTH (MILES)	DIFFICULTY/ ELEVATION	HIGHLIGHTS
8 Palo Duro Canyon PAGE 92	Amarillo	5	Challenging 777'	Canyon, rock formations, scenic views, big sky
9 Caprock Canyons PAGE 96	Amarillo / Lubbock	3.5	Challenging 449'	Cave, scenic views, canyon, big sky, bison
10 Big Cave PAGE 100	Amarillo	2	Moderate 177'	Cave, rock formations, big sky
11 Elm Creek PAGE 104	Abilene	2	Easy 42'	Creek, wildlife

ADVENTURES IN
HILL COUNTRY

ADVENTURE	HUB	LENGTH (MILES)	DIFFICULTY/ ELEVATION	HIGHLIGHTS
12 Old Baldy PAGE 110	Austin / San Antonio	1	Challenging 439'	Summit, scenic views
13 Crystal Cave PAGE 114	Austin	1.5	Challenging 403'	Cave, wildlife
14 Monkey Rock PAGE 118	San Antonio	4.4	Challenging 561'	Cool rocks, scenic view, canyon, wildflowers

ADVENTURE	HUB	LENGTH (MILES)	DIFFICULTY/ ELEVATION	HIGHLIGHTS
15 Enchanted Rock PAGE 122	Austin / San Antonio	3.4	Challenging 593'	Huge granite dome, giant boulders, history, summit
16 Gorman Falls PAGE 126	Austin	2.8	Challenging 331'	Waterfall
17 Devil's Backbone PAGE 130	Austin	3.4	Moderate 190'	Swimming hole, granite hills, waterfall
18 Reimers Ranch PAGE 134	Austin / San Antonio	1.9	Moderate 144'	Rocky cliffs, river, swimming hole
19 Pedernales Falls PAGE 138	Austin / San Antonio	1.7	Moderate 150'	Waterfall, rocky moonscape, river
20 Guadalupe River PAGE 142	San Antonio	1.6	Easy 95'	River, swimming hole, birds
21 Central Texas Tropics PAGE 146	Austin / San Antonio	3.1	Easy 45'	Tropical plants, boardwalk
22 Lockhart Loop PAGE 150	Austin / San Antonio	1.2	Easy 115'	Waterfall, wildlife
23 Lower Falls PAGE 154	Austin	3.2	Moderate 194'	Waterfall, rock overhang, history
24 Garey Park PAGE 158	Austin	1.4	Easy 45'	Rock formations, river, birds
25 Crockett Gardens Falls PAGE 162	Austin	3.7	Moderate 321'	Waterfall, swimming area, limestone cliffs
26 Berry Springs Park PAGE 166	Austin	1	Easy 16'	Pond, donkeys, history

ADVENTURES IN
PRAIRIES AND LAKES

ADVENTURE	HUB	LENGTH (MILES)	DIFFICULTY/ ELEVATION	HIGHLIGHTS
27 Chalk Ridge Falls PAGE 172	Austin	1.2	Moderate 90'	Waterfall, suspension bridge
28 Cave, Tower, and Pond Loop PAGE 176	Austin	1.4	Easy 118'	Cave, tower, pond
29 Dinosaur Valley PAGE 180	Dallas / Fort Worth	2	Moderate 160'	Dinosaur tracks, history, river, limestone ledges
30 Penitentiary Hollow PAGE 184	Dallas / Fort Worth	1.2	Moderate 187'	Rock formations, lake
31 Huck Finn Trail PAGE 188	Dallas / Fort Worth	1.1	Easy 55'	Waterfall, cool bridge, turtles
32 Cattail Pond PAGE 192	Dallas / Fort Worth	2.5	Challenging 321'	Pond, wildlife, birds, butterflies
33 Lake Somerville PAGE 196	Austin / Houston	2.1	Easy 18'	Lake, eagles

ADVENTURES IN
THE PINEY WOODS

ADVENTURE	HUB	LENGTH (MILES)	DIFFICULTY/ ELEVATION	HIGHLIGHTS
34 Tall Trees of Texas PAGE 202	Dallas / Fort Worth	1.3	Easy 121'	Waterfall, tall trees, wildlife
35 Rustling Leaves PAGE 206	Dallas / Fort Worth	1.4	Easy 118'	Tall trees, lake
36 Caddo Forest Trail PAGE 210	Dallas / Fort Worth	1.5	Easy 183'	Tall trees
37 Historic Sawmill Ruins PAGE 214	Houston	4.9	Challenging 121'	Waterfall, history, tall trees
38 Davy Crockett National Forest PAGE 218	Houston	2.8	Easy 137'	Tall trees, lake, boardwalk, wildlife
39 CCC Bathtubs PAGE 222	Houston	1.2	Easy / 200'	Tall trees, history
40 Lone Star Hiking Trail PAGE 226	Houston	2.4	Easy 56'	History, lake, tall trees
41 Pineywoods Boardwalk PAGE 230	Houston	1	Easy 13'	Boardwalk, tall trees, wildlife viewing, pond
42 Carnivorous Plants PAGE 234	Houston	1	Easy 22'	Carnivorous plants, tall trees, boardwalk

ADVENTURES IN
THE COASTAL PLAINS

ADVENTURE	HUB	LENGTH (MILES)	DIFFICULTY/ ELEVATION	HIGHLIGHTS
43 Sheldon Lake State Park PAGE 240	Houston	1.8	Easy 6'	Alligators, observation tower, boardwalk
44 El Franco Lee Park PAGE 244	Houston	2.1	Easy 16'	Birds, butterflies, gazebo
45 40 Acre Lake Trail PAGE 248	Houston	1.2	Easy 26'	Alligators, birds, observation tower, lake
46 Brazos River PAGE 252	Houston	2.1	Easy 46'	River, wildlife
47 Lake Corpus Christi PAGE 256	Corpus Christi	2.5	Easy 75'	Lake, history
48 Malaquite Beach Walk PAGE 260	Corpus Christi	2.4	Easy 0'	Beach, birds
49 Resaca PAGE 264	Corpus Christi	4.0	Easy (with tram); Challenging (without tram) / 36'	Birds, tram
50 Rio Grande Valley PAGE 268	Corpus Christi	1.4	Easy 9'	Alligators, birds, pond

Exploring the cave at Caprock Canyons

ADVENTURES BY FEATURE

Can you remember the first cave you explored? The first waterfall that misted your face? Each of these adventures includes a destination or item of particular interest to motivate young legs and reward hard work. Encourage kids, as co-adventurers, to talk about which types of natural features tickle them the most and why.

FEATURE	ADVENTURE
Lakes and ponds	25 Lake Georgetown
	32 Cattail Pond
	33 Lake Somerville
	35 Lake at Rustling Leaves
	36 Lake at Caddo Forest Trail
	38 Lake at Davey Crockett National Forest
	39 CCC bathtubs
	40 Lake at Lone Star Hiking Trail
	41 Lake at Pineywoods Boardwalk
	43 Lake at Sheldon Rocks State Park
	47 Lake Corpus Christi
	50 Pond at Rio Grande Valley
Waterfall	16 Gorman Falls
	17 Waterfall at Devil's Backbone
	19 Pedernales Falls
	23 Lower Falls
	25 Crockett Gardens Falls
	27 Chalk Ridge Falls
	31 Waterfall at Huck Finn Trail
	34 Rock waterfall at Tall Trees of Texas
History	7 Pump jacks and windmills at Monahans Sandhills
	13 CCC pavilion and dance floor at Crystal Cave
	22 CCC recreation hall and water tower at Lockhart Loop
	23 Homestead and gristmill ruins at Lower Falls
	26 Historic compound at Berry Springs Park
	29 Dinosaur tracks at Dinosaur Valley
	30 Cattle thieves at Penitentiary Hollow

FEATURE	ADVENTURE
History *(cont'd)*	**35** CCC grill at Rustling Leaves
	37 Historic Sawmill Ruins
	39 CCC bathtubs
	46 Texas history at Brazos River
Flora and fauna	**3** Black bears at Basin Loop Trail
	4 Montezuma Quail
	6 Javelinas at Smith Spring
	9 Bison and prairie dogs at Caprock Canyons
	11 Birds at Elm Creek
	21 Tropical plants at Central Texas Tropics
	23 500-year-old tree at Lower Falls
	24 Bluebirds at Garey Park
	33 Bald eagles at Lake Somerville
	34 Tall Trees of Texas
	42 Carnivorous Plants
	43 Alligators at Sheldon Lake State Park
	44 Birds at El Franco Lee
	48 Birds at Malaquite Beach
	49 Birds at Resaca de la Palma State Park
	50 Alligators at Rio Grande Valley
Geology	**2** Pouroff at Lower Burro Mesa
	4 Igneous rock formations at Montezuma Quail Trail
	5 Mitre Peak and Sleeping Lion Formation at Chihuahuan Desert
	7 Sand dunes at Monahans Sandhills
	8 Rock garden at Palo Duro Canyon
	9 Natural bridge at Caprock Canyons
	12 Old Baldy

FEATURE	ADVENTURE
Geology *(cont'd)*	**14** Monkey Rock
	15 Large granite dome and Turkey Peak at Enchanted Rock
	17 Gneiss rock and pink granite at Devil's Backbone
	18 Climber's Canyon at Reimers Ranch
	19 Pedernales Falls
	23 Rock shelter and limestone moonscape at Lower Falls
	24 Brain Rock at Garey Park
	29 Dinosaur tracks at Dinosaur Valley
	30 Limestone canyon at Penitentiary Hollow
Caves	**9** Natural bridge cave at Caprock Canyons
	10 Big Cave
	13 Crystal Cave
	19 Grotto at Pedernales Falls
	28 Tonkawa Cave at Cave, Tower, and Pond Loop
Summits and peaks	**3** Basin Loop Trail
	8 Palo Duro Canyon
	12 Old Baldy
	15 Enchanted Rock
River exploration	**1** Rio Grande at Santa Elena Canyon
	11 Elm Creek
	14 Sabinal River at Monkey Rock
	16 Colorado River at Gorman Falls
	17 Colorado River at Devil's Backbone
	18 Pedernales River at Reimers Ranch
	19 Pedernales River at Pedernales Falls

FEATURE	ADVENTURE
River exploration (cont'd)	**20** Guadalupe River
	21 San Marcos River at Central Texas Tropics
	23 Onion Creek at Lower Falls
	24 San Gabriel River at Garey Park
	27 Lampasas River at Chalk Ridge Falls
	28 Leon River at Cave, Tower, and Pond Loop
	29 Paluxy River at Dinosaur Valley
	31 Prairie Creek at Huck Finn Trail
Beach fun	**12** Frio River at Old Baldy
	20 Pebble beach at Guadalupe River
	30 Sandy swimming area at Penitentiary Hollow
	48 Malaquite Beach
Campground by trailhead	**1** Cottonwood near Santa Elena Canyon
	2 Chisos Basin near Lower Burro Mesa Pouroff
	3 Chisos Basin near Basin Loop Trail
	4 Davis Mountain State Park at Montezuma Quail Trail
	6 Pine Springs near Smith Spring
	7 Willow Draw near Monahans Sandhills
	9 Honey Flat at Caprock Canyons
	10 Wolfberry Group Camp near Big Cave
	11 Wagon Circle and Oak Grove near Elm Creek
	12 Pecan Grove or Oakmont near Old Baldy and Crystal Cave

FEATURE	ADVENTURE
Campground by trailhead *(cont'd)*	14 Lost Maples Campground by Monkey Rock
	15 Enchanted Rock State Park
	16 North Camping Area at Gorman Falls
	17 Inks Lake State Park by Devil's Backbone
	19 Pedernales Falls State Park
	20 Cedar Sage by Guadalupe River
	21 Palmetto State Park near Central Texas Tropics
	22 Clear Fork Creek by Lockhart Loop
	23 Big Oak by Lower Falls
	26 Berry Springs Park
	28 Mother Neff State Park by Cove, Tower, and Pond Loop
	29 Dinosaur Valley State Park
	30 Lake Mineral Wells State Park by Penitentiary Hollow
	33 Birch Creek Unit by Lake Somerville
	34 Tyler State Park by Tall Trees of Texas
	35 Daingerfield State Park by Rustling Leaves
	36 Caddo Lake State Park
	37 Carney Creek near Sawmill Ruins
	38 Ratcliff Lake Recreation Area by Davy Crockett National Forest
	39 Mission Tejas State Park by CCC Bathtubs
	40 Double Lake Recreation Area by Lone Star Hiking Trail
	41 Lake Livingston State Park by Pineywoods Boardwalk
	45 Brazos Bend State Park by 40 Acre Lake Trail
	46 Stephen F. Austin State Park by Brazos River
	47 Lake Corpus Christi State Park
	48 Malaquite Campground by Malaquite Beach Walk

ADVENTURES BY SEASON

Texans are lucky to enjoy year-round outdoor adventure, with mild winters and plenty of swimming holes to stay cool in summer. Spring is often thought to be the best time for outdoor adventuring in Texas. The temperatures are perfect, wildflowers are in bloom, and migrant birds are arriving. As the temperatures begin to heat up in the summer months, hiking becomes more of a challenge. We like to plan hikes that double as swimming holes so that we can take a dip before or during the hike to cool off. Always bring plenty of water and a sports drink to replace electrolytes, and pay attention to excessive heat warnings issued by parks. Consider hiking early in the morning or late in the afternoon to beat the heat. Fall is another beautiful hiking season in Texas as the temperatures begin to cool. There are several places in Texas where you can enjoy colorful displays of fall foliage, from the crown jewel of Lost Maples State Natural Area, to the Piney Woods of East Texas, to the bald cypress trees lining the rivers of the Hill Country. As winter approaches and the temperatures cool again, Texas offers a variety of weather conditions, from sunny and mild to snowy and cold. Winter visitors to South Padre Island can enjoy average highs of 70 degrees, while winter visitors to the Panhandle Plains may be in for a winter wonderland, with snowy canyon views stretching as far as the eye can see.

When possible, try visiting the same places during different times of year. Encourage your kids to understand the seasons by returning to a favorite hike at different times of the year and posing the question: What has changed since your last visit?

Texas summer hiking tip: Find a park that doubles as a swimming hole, like Dinosaur Valley State Park

FEATURE	ADVENTURE
Winter	**8** Palo Duro Canyon
	10 Big Cave
	41 Pineywoods Boardwalk
Spring	**1/2** Santa Elena Canyon and Lower Burro Mesa Pouroff Trail
	9 Caprock Canyons
	15 Enchanted Rock
	16 Gorman Falls
	19 Pedernales Falls
	24 Garey Park
	26 Berry Springs Park
	28 Cave, Tower, and Pond Loop
	31 Huck Finn Trail
	32 Cattail Pond
	33 Lake Somerville
	40 Lone Star Hiking Trail
	42 Carnivorous Plants
	43 Sheldon Lake State Park
	44 El Franco Lee Park
	45 40 Acre Lake Trail
	46 Brazos River
	47 Lake Corpus Christi
	49 Resaca

Summer		
	(4)	Montezuma Quail Trail
	(5)	Chihuahuan Sky Island
	(13)	Crystal Cave
	(17)	Devil's Backbone
	(18)	Reimers Ranch
	(19)	Pedernales Falls
	(20)	Guadalupe River
	(21)	Central Texas Tropics
	(22)	Lockhart Loop
	(23)	Lower Falls
	(24)	Garey Park
	(25)	Crockett Gardens Falls
	(27)	Chalk Ridge Falls
	(29)	Dinosaur Valley
	(30)	Penitentiary Hollow
	(48)	Malaquite Beach Walk
	(50)	Rio Grande Valley

Fall		
	(3)	Basin Loop Trail
	(6)	Smith Spring
	(7)	Monahans Sandhills
	(11)	Elm Creek
	(14)	Monkey Rock
	(34)	Tall Trees of Texas
	(35)	Rustling Leaves
	(36)	Caddo Forest Trail
	(37)	Historic Sawmill Ruins
	(38)	Davy Crockett National Forest
	(39)	CCC Bathtubs

PREPARING FOR YOUR ADVENTURE

A great trail is a story—it has a beginning, a climax or crux, and then an end, whether back the way you came or wrapping up in a loop. As you read the maps with your children, encourage them to feel the story of the trail. How did you like the beginning? What was the crux? How did it end? What characters were on the trail? Which trees or animals stood out to them? A fun after-hike activity is taking your nature journal and writing a fictional account of what happened on the trail, making the landscape come alive in a whole new way.

INDIVIDUAL ADVENTURE PROFILES

This guide is a starter pack for a life full of adventure with your young ones. As they grow bigger and stronger, they will be ready for more challenging adventures such as hiking 8.5 miles round trip with a 3000-foot elevation gain to reach a West Texas gem—Guadalupe Peak, the highest point in Texas. In the meantime, work together to taste what each spectacularly diverse region has to offer and note which to return to in the future.

We've organized this guide as a west-to-east journey. We begin in West Texas and Big Bend Country and finish off with the Piney Woods of Texas and the Coastal Plains. In the middle we will journey through the Panhandle Plains, the Hill Country, and the Prairies and Lakes Region.

Each of the fifty adventure profiles includes a basic trail map and information on the species of plants and wildlife, points of historic interest, and geological features that you may see on the trail. By allowing children to navigate using the maps and route-elevation guides, read the hike and species descriptions, and look for each featured item like a scavenger hunt, you're fostering the building blocks of adventure. Marking journeys on the map with these points of interest gives relevance and context to kids' surroundings, so encourage them to note areas that stood out to them as well. You'll burst with pride when they start to teach you what a lollipop loop is versus an out-and-back, or when they're able to gauge whether they are happy with a hike with 200 feet of elevation gain or want to tackle 1000. They'll learn to make decisions about their own adventure trail. Each entry is written for both you and the kids, so encourage them to read to themselves or out loud to you.

Elevation profile, length, type of trail, and time

The elevation-profile graph is a line that sketches the general arc of the up-and-down during the hike. You'll notice a few are almost completely flat, while others are nearly a triangle. The elevation listed is how many feet you'll gain from start to finish; so even if it rolls up and then down again, if it says 300 feet that will be the total number of feet you'll climb from the trailhead to the summit. No adventure is less than a mile, which would be too short to be called a real excursion, or more than 5 miles, a distance that might be too taxing for younger or newer adventurers. The length of these hikes should give you plenty of time to enjoy the outing before anyone gets too tired. Embracing shorter trails translates into more time to savor them. Some of the routes are shorter versions of a longer or different available route and are modified for kids. Also, we always note whether the adventure is an out-and-back, a loop, or a lollipop loop and whether a clockwise or counterclockwise route is recommended.

 An out-and-back has a clear final destination and turnaround point; you'll cross back over what you've already covered.

 A loop provides brand-new territory the whole way around.

A lollipop is a straight line with a mini-loop at the end, like reaching a lake and then circling it and heading back.

Talking with kids about the type of trail you're planning to hike will help young adventurers know what's coming and what to expect. The estimated hike time includes time for exploration. Give yourselves the delight of a relaxing hike with plenty of time to stop and play with a pile of fun-looking rocks, have leaf-boat races on a stream, or sketch a bird.

Level of difficulty

This rating system was designed to facilitate having a good time. It's important to note that these are kid-centric ratings; what's labeled as a "challenging" trail in this guide may not appear to be so challenging to a seasoned adult hiker. It can be fun to create your own rating for a trail when you're finished. "Did that feel like a level 1, 2, or 3 to you? Why?" Talking about it can help you understand their adventure limits or help them seek new challenges. None of the trails in this book are paved (at least not all the way), but some are level and smooth, and due to the geological history of Texas, most have some combination of rocks and roots. There will be notes if there are steep sections where you'll want to hold smaller hands. The rockier terrain will necessitate some sturdy shoes, while the river exploration may call for a pair of sturdy water sandals. You'll want to have a sense of the local landscape and your own child's preferences to inform your decision of which type will be best for your kid.

Check reviews, if you wish, on AllTrails.com to get recent conditions and other families' opinions of the difficulty. While scouting these trails, we saw many walking toddlers and strollers of every tire type imaginable, including a couple of sport strollers on moderately rocky trails with exposed roots. We also saw baby backpacks on even the most challenging terrain. Use the information here to make informed decisions.

The adventures are rated as follows:

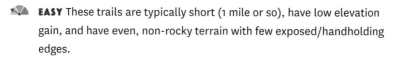 **EASY** These trails are typically short (1 mile or so), have low elevation gain, and have even, non-rocky terrain with few exposed/handholding edges.

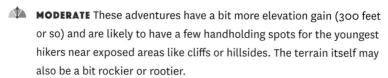 **MODERATE** These adventures have a bit more elevation gain (300 feet or so) and are likely to have a few handholding spots for the youngest hikers near exposed areas like cliffs or hillsides. The terrain itself may also be a bit rockier or rootier.

CHALLENGING These adventures will give your little adventurers the biggest sense of accomplishment. These have the most elevation gain (300 to 1000 feet) or sections where you'll probably want to keep kids close as they take in an exposed view. However, if the hike is steeper, it'll also be shorter—more than doable with the right attitude and by taking advantage of power-up stops and the adrenaline-inducing rush of finding special scavenger-hunt items.

Season

This section lists the season when the adventure is possible; in many cases, the trails can be hiked year-round. Seasons when features of special interest can be seen, such as wildflowers or rushing waterfalls, are noted. In winter and early spring, check with the local agency listed for each hike to make sure the trail and access road is actually open. In general, the higher up you go, the more likely you could be closed out by snow on either side of summer. Some adventures lend themselves to snow exploration without any gear, though, and others are a great time to try snowshoes or snow tracks (Yaktrax) on your shoes if you're so inclined.

Phenology is the study of how plants change across the seasons, and hikers are often the first to notice when leaves change colors or when a certain flower starts to bloom. Try taking the same hike in different seasons so your young hikers can learn about how things, especially flora and fauna, change over the course of a year. Plus, the more often you go, the more likely you are to find something you may have missed the last time.

Get there

When my co-author, Wendy Gorton, was seven, her dad took their family out for their first off-roading experience in a small white Toyota pickup in the California desert. Their truck was promptly lodged between two rocks and got towed out six hours later. Although that experience built some character and an adventurous spirit in her, these kinds of roads are not included in this guide. These Texas adventures have all been road-tested at least once and specifically target trailheads with fairly easy access, meaning minimal dirt, gravel, or pothole-strewn roads (we'll leave those to seasoned adventurers).

Luckily, long drives are sometimes spiced up with wildlife, like this bison crossing

Texas is big, y'all. Over 268,000 square miles. This guide is meant to be a promotion for the diverse and beautiful areas throughout the state. We hope that you and your children flip through and dream of one day taking a road trip to hike to the rim of the second largest canyon in the United States at Palo Duro Canyon, summit the pink granite batholith at Enchanted Rock, or birdwatch at the southernmost tip of Texas. Car rides are a necessity to reach the amazing buffet of hikes available to you, Texans. We hope you'll embrace the special family time that road trips can offer your crew.

Of course you have your screen of choice, but consider a few fun ways to make the hours fly, by such as riddles, the A-Z game (you claim every time you see something that starts with the next letter of the alphabet), audio Harry Potter books, call-and-response-type camp songs (bit.ly/TimberSongs), nature journaling, and just good old-fashioned conversation. Always be ready to roll down windows for fresh air, and encourage your little riders to focus on the horizon if they start to get carsick. We encourage you to make the most of every trip—always stop by visitor centers, and consider extending an outing into a camping trip.

Each adventure comes with a case-sensitive Google Maps link you can drop directly into your browser to access directions to the trailhead on your smartphone. Just be sure to do this before you head out while you are still certain to have coverage. You can also download offline maps with Google Maps and the AllTrails app for free, which will allow you to follow your GGPS dot and ensure you're staying on the right trail or road. Basic longhand directions to each trailhead are also provided. You can also get free highway maps mailed to you or printed, which can be helpful and educational for your copilot in the car (check the state tourism website, TravelTexas.com). You can also geek out with the kids on Google Earth or use satellite view on Google Maps to preview your road (and sometimes even trail) step-by-step.

There's something magical about maps, and each physical map in this guide was carefully designed with kids in mind to be touched, traced, and held out in front of them to understand the land around them. Encourage them to understand the difference between roads, highways, and interstates. Even numbers, for instance, run east and west, while odds run north and south. We've simplified the maps so kids can focus on the land agencies they'll be visiting, the nearby cities, town, and kid-worthy landmarks, like caves, bridges, benches and more. Hopefully they start to build a sixth sense of understanding how to navigate using maps while they adventure with you. How long will this adventure take, do you think? Where does that river start, and how far does it have to go to get to the ocean? How many turns will we need to make? What's our next highway? Any cities nearby? Any fun names you can see? Just by asking questions you can encourage curiosity and leadership with your young adventurers.

Restrooms

We can't have a hiking book for kids without chatting about bathrooms. Many of the trails have pit toilets or developed toilets right at the parking lot. If not, plan on a restroom stop in the nearest town or gas station on your way in and on your way out. Discuss appropriate trail bathroom etiquette with your kids as well, such as heading safely off the trail, away from water, and properly covering it should the need arise. Bring what you need to be comfortable in your adventure pack, such as a Ziploc bag with toilet paper. Don't leave any toilet paper behind to spoil someone else's experience— always pack it out.

Parking and fees

Your main goal, lead adventurers, is to get out on the trail. If thinking about how to park and pay gets your boot laces knotted up, rest assured that as long as you have some cash or a card in the glove compartment, the team will be just fine. All the trailheads listed here have a parking lot or pull-out and some sort of trail sign indicating where you are and whether you need a parking pass or permit. For some, you'll need to plan ahead and get a day-use pass or annual pass before you get to the trailhead. Others have self-service pay stations at the trailhead—either those accepting credit cards or an "iron ranger" with a slot in it for a fee envelope with cash or check—and you'll affix the pass to your car. Some parking lots are free, though, and those are noted. There are several "fee-free days," including National Public Lands Day in September and many holidays. A Texas State Parks annual pass is $70—well worth it! We were able to witness firsthand during winter how the staff and rangers keep trails safe and at the ready for us and our families, and these fees pay for that maintenance.

A well-earned cool treat ends the adventure on a high note

Treat yourself

To reward yourselves, the guide lists nearby cafes and restaurants for good, quick bites, in part so you can plan whether you need to pack substantial snacks or just a few with you on the trail. These are road-tested yummy bakeries, ice cream shops, burger joints, and family-friendly breweries with notable items or spaces that your kids will enjoy. Texas's bounty of barbecue, sweet and savory kolaches, chili con queso, breakfast tacos, and pecan pie spice up every new corner of the state you explore.

Managing agencies

The name of the agency that manages each of the hiking trails is given, along with its telephone number and Facebook handle (which is also usually its Twitter and Instagram handle). Before heading out, it's a good idea to check on current conditions, including weather, roads, wildlife sightings, and any hazards that haven't been cleared or fixed. The folks on the other end are often rangers and are generally thrilled to share information about their trails. They also can connect you to botanists, geologists, historians, and more. Involve your kids by encouraging them to say hello and to ask about conditions or an unanswered question on the trail.

Scavenger hunts

The scavenger hunt in each adventure invites you to look for specific fungi, plants, animals, minerals, geological formations, and historical items of interest. You'll find descriptions and photos of trees, leaves, flowers, seeds, cones, bark, nuts, wildlife or animal tracks, fur and feathers, as well as details about rocks and geological features, historically significant land-marks or artifacts, natural features such as lakes and rivers and waterfalls, or culturally significant spots that appear on each trail. Each entry has a question to ponder or an activity to try, and when applicable, you can dig into the scientific genus and species and learn the very beginnings of how classification works, and why the plant or animal is called what it is. Encourage kids to "preview" what they might see on the trail, and if they think they've found it, take out the map to match. Take it up a notch and encourage them to make their own scavenger hunt—write down five things they think they might see on the trail today, from very basic (five different kinds of trees) to very specific (five loblolly pine cones on the ground).

IDENTIFYING WHAT YOU FIND

Identifying these species in the wild involves using clues from size, leaves, bark, flowers, and the habitat. Work with kids to ask questions that will move them from general identification (Is it a conifer or a deciduous tree?) to the specifics (What shape are the leaves? What species is this?). The species of trees, shrubs, mushrooms, wildflowers, and animals listed in the scavenger hunts were chosen because you should be able to find them with ease and because there's something interesting about them that might appeal to children. You may not find every species on the trail every time, however. It's best to adopt the attitude of considering it a win when you do, and consider those you can't find as something to look for next time.

Tristan Gooley, British author of *The Natural Navigator*, encourages kids to look for "keys" as they walk on trails. "Keys are small families of

What is "the tree with knees"? Help your young hikers figure it out.

Because of its size and geography, Texas is one of the most biologically diverse states in the United States, hosting plants in forests, deserts, mountains, hills, prairies, and coastal plains. In fact, Texas boasts over 5000 species of native plants and almost 400 of these species occur nowhere else but Texas. That's what makes Texas special.

—Meg Inglis, Native Plant Society of Texas

clues and signs. If we focus on them repeatedly, it can give us a sixth sense." For example, start noticing where the sun is when you start and when you end and where the natural features (hills, mountains) are around you. Bring along an actual compass or use the compass on your smartphone to start understanding direction.

When you find a particularly interesting species on the trail that's not mentioned in the scavenger hunt, have kids either sketch or take a photo of it. Remind them to look it up later, either in a printed field guide to the region or on a specialty website such as WildflowerSearch.com.

Other ID options include using Google Image Search (drop in your snapshot and compare it to similar images) or looking it up on iNaturalist.org. Adding basic descriptions and the name of the region can help narrow your search in online field guides.

To treasure-hunt species while on the trail, download the Seek by iNaturalist or LeafSnap apps.

If you're ready to level up everyone's identification skills, join the Native Plant Society of Texas (NPSOT.org). This is a great place to learn about plants that have evolved naturally in your region of Texas. Native plants do not need special treatment to thrive, they are the best source of food for wildlife, and they make your region look like "home." Join over 3000 members and help spread the word about the importance and benefits of native plants. They have great Facebook groups and newsletters for each region where you can share when species start to bloom or a photo of a species you can't identify. Joining your local chapter also means getting invited to their fun group hikes on themes such as wildflowers or fungi and everything in between. You'll be exposing your kids to the power of a community resource where everyone is passionate about nature and science and wants to help each other out.

There's even the Central and North Texas Mycological Societies (CentralTexasMycology.org and NorthTexasMycology.org) and the National Speleological Society (for cavers!) you can join. The USA National Phenology Network (USANPN.org) allows kids to contribute to actual science by entering their observation of seasonal changes into a nation-wide database, and it has a cool

Look at the things you encounter from different scales and from different angles and different parts. For example, a tree—you have a really large organism and you might need to stand really far away to see a picture of it. But look closer—find the fruit on the ground, look at the bark, and look at the leaves. Think of all of the different characteristics that can help you learn what it is, why it lives where it does. Start recognizing all of the pieces of an organism and thinking how to best capture those photographically if you want to share your record with the world. Try to find the part of the thing that is most unique-looking and try to fill the frame with a nice, clear photo of that feature.

—Carrie Seltzer, iNaturalist

My grandfather was a naturalist, my dad was a geologist, and now so is my son. When out in nature or driving and we see a cinder cone, we wonder together why rocks look like toothpaste in an outcrop and why are houses being inundated with water? It's these observational things that make us all curious and that lead us to ask questions. "Why?" is the true question of science. That's what brings us into geology—observing and wondering why. That's the beautiful part about this science. Most of time is not represented in rock—we make inferences and guesses. If your kids know that you don't know the answer either, you can explore together. You can ask: What do you think that little thing means? Why is it bent? Why is it a certain color? Why does this rock that looks so different lie next to this rock? Why is this so soft, and this so hard? Next thing you know, they're learning mineralogy and stratigraphy without even saying those words. It's great problem-solving for your kids, a four-dimensional puzzle.

—Scott W. Tinker, State Geologist of Texas

Junior Phenologist Program and kid-friendly resources to boot.

While encountering these cool colors, folds, and structures, encourage children to think about the general rock cycle—a rock's evolution from igneous (melted rock) to metamorphic to sedimentary—and how it builds up in deposits over time. Use the scavenger hunts to start to build a familiarity with Texas' many layers so your kids can start to find them and notice their subtle differences.

Join a regional geological society like the Geological Societies for South, West, East, and North Texas, as well as for Houston and Austin (STGS.org, WTGS.org, EastTexasGeo.com, NTGeologicalSociety.org, HGS.org, AustinGeoSoc.org) for newsletters, group hikes, and community opportunities. Feel free to pick up and investigate the different rocks you find, scratching them to see what happens and sketching them in your nature journal.

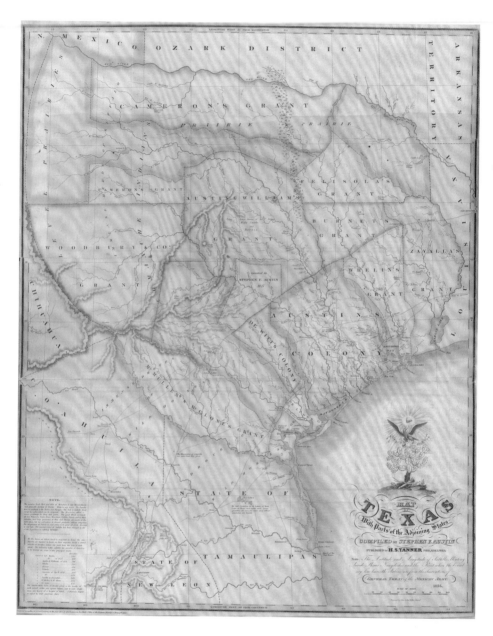

Stephen F. Austin's 1830 map of Texas—how does it differ
from today's map? How have things changed?

As young people go and hike, they should think about who came first. Which Native Americans were here in this region, in East Texas, South Texas, or the Panhandle? How did they survive here? If you pay attention, you learn many things; many times when you're on these hiking trails, you might run into people. You'll never know if you're on the same trail with a Federal Judge, or you stop at a shady spot and find out someone is from Europe and has a whole different perspective. Take these opportunities to visit with new people and engage with them in the beauty of the surroundings. Talk to your grandparents and parents to find out your own personal history, because that will give you passion to connect to the broader world and preserve your own little history.

—Monte L. Monroe, Texas State Historian

HISTORICAL ITEMS

There are often items of historical interest on Texas trails. Join the Texas State Historical Association (TSHAOnline.org), then be sure to look for the larger city near you as they often have their own and can have cool archives and photos from the past. Adults can foster inquiry with each hike.

POWER-UP STOPS

Liz Thomas has hiked over 15,000 miles and is the former speed record holder for the Appalachian Trail in the United States. Her biggest tip for young adventurers to build stamina? "Understand your body. Kids are just figuring out how to read their bodies. You can think of your body as having gauges and you're the pilot at the front of the plane. Your goal is to keep your gauges (hydration, exposure, food) in the happy zone." She even sets reminders on her watch to drink and eat as she walks from sunrise to sunset. As lead adventurers, you'll be keeping a close eye on these gauges but also teaching your kids to recognize, anticipate, and power through them.

APPRECIATING THE WORK OF THE CCC

Before we go another step, we must acknowledge the important contributions of the Civilian Conservation Corps (the CCC) here in Texas in times past. President Franklin D. Roosevelt and the U.S. Congress created this group in 1933 to provide jobs on public lands for unemployed people, specifically young men and World War I veterans. Well into the early 1940s, these crews worked on over 30 Texas state parks. The companies were segregated by race. The CCC program no longer exists, and conservation groups, thankfully, have not been segregated for decades.

The crews created and installed substantial features, from roads and trails to shelters, dams, water towers, and observation towers—even swimming pools and dance pavilions! Many of these remain in use or are still standing today and are included in a number of our favorite adventures in these pages. Be sure to admire their hard work. Thank you, CCC!

Sometimes power-ups are a great chance to let children play and explore, like climbing the enticing rocks you'll come across

For each adventure, we note key places that serve as mini-milestones, or power-up stops. Be sure to pack snacks for your kid to eat at these stops to keep blood sugar, energy levels, and mood high. Remember that this amount of physical activity may be challenging for little ones. Often, the power-up stops are at points of interest: fun bridges, switchbacks before a small hill, or an overlook with a view. Stopping for a moment can fuel you up, give you a chance to listen to the wind or birds, watch what's going on in the woods, and prepare you for the larger goal of finishing the adventure itself.

Power-up stops can also be great for a nursing mom or a bottle-feeding dad or partner, or for tending to other little ones' needs, as well as for question-based games like "I Spy." As the lead adventurers, use these stops for inspiration, play, questions, games, and riddles and encourage your kids to do the same. Don't underestimate the power of choosing a special snack to serve as a particular motivator on tough ascents or rainy days.

ADVENTURE BAG, SUPPLIES, AND SAFETY

A couple of young adventurers with adventure bags in tow

Start your kids on a lifelong habit of packing an adventure bag, whether it's the smallest satchel or the largest consumer-grade backpack they can actually hold or tote on their back. It's a great way to introduce them to self-sufficiency.

The art of having everything you need along without being overly burdened is key to having a good time on the trail. All of the adventures in this guide are short enough that even if you did pack too much, its weight won't jeopardize your enjoyment levels. Review the trail location, its length, and proximity to town and decide what your team needs to feel comfortable and safe. REI (Recreational Equipment, Inc.) recommends the following 10 essentials.

 NAVIGATION Keep your smartphone charged for access to offline maps and the compass feature. The free version of the AllTrails app includes maps of hiking trails accessible online so that you can make sure you're on the right track in real time. The paid version of the app allows you to access offline maps to track your hike and help navigate areas without internet service. The free Texas State Parks app is also a great source of information about each state park, including directions, current alerts, a short video tour, and the option to reserve a site.

HYDRATION Bring plenty of water for everyone. For most of the hikes in this book during most of the year, one liter of water per person per hike will suffice. That means a family of four should bring at least a gallon of drinking water on a hike. For hot summer days or longer hikes, plan on more, at least one gallon of water per person, plus a sports drink or snack to replace lost electrolytes. Some of these trails are fairly exposed, so if you choose to go in the warmer time of the year, go early or late in the day and be sure to bring proper sunscreen and hats/protective clothing.

On hot summer weekends at the most popular parks, it's not uncommon to have several heat rescues per day. Many of these are pet-related, so if you like to hike with an adventure pup like we do, make sure you take their needs into account. Unless the hike is along an accessible water source, dogs need their own water bottle and bowl to stay hydrated. Remember that dogs cannot regulate their body temperature as effectively as humans can (they cannot sweat!).

NUTRITION Consider the length of the trail and the amount and type of snacks you'll need to keep the train going. Snacks with protein and fat are important on long hikes, while carbs provide quick energy bursts. A sweet treat can be a fun celebration when you reach a key milestone during the hike or can bring out some renewed enthusiasm when morale is starting to wane.

FIRE Pack a lighter or matchbook for emergencies.

FIRST AID KIT This can range from a mini first aid kit with essentials such as bandages and aspirin to much heftier options with space blankets. Consider what you want your car stocked with and what you want on the trail.

TOOLS A small knife or multi-tool goes a long way in the woods.

ILLUMINATION Did you explore just a wee bit too long and dusk is approaching? A simple headlamp, flashlight, or even your phone's flashlight can help lead the way.

SUN AND INSECT PROTECTION If it's an exposed trail, consider sunglasses and sunscreen and/or hats for you and the kids. In the summer, many trails may have mosquitoes, so be prepared with your preferred method of repelling them.

SHELTER You may want a space blanket or small tarp in your adventure bag in case of emergency.

INSULATION Check the weather together and decide on the type of protection and warmth you want to bring. A second layer is always a good idea; breezes can chill even the warmest of days, and Texas' late-summer thunderstorms can sneak up and bring cool temperatures and downpours.

Lenore Skenazy, president of Let Grow (a nonprofit promoting independence as a critical part of childhood) and founder of the Free-Range Kids Movement, has this reply about handling the inevitable fear of shepherding your family:

I'm often asked, "What if something goes wrong?" I love to ask back, "Can anyone remember something that went wrong when you were a kid, playing with other kids?" People often look back so fondly on that time. There's even a word for the way we treasure imperfect things and moments: wabi-sabi, *from the Japanese practice of filling a crack in a vase—an imperfection—with gold, because the imperfection is what makes it beautiful. The outdoors is never without some surprises and even minor risks, but neither is the indoors. My guess is you all can remember when something went wrong and it is a treasured (if only in retrospect!) memory. Imperfection is inevitable and valuable. Be brave, be resourceful, and stay calm!*

Power-ups are perfect opportunities to stop and hydrate

Fun items to have on hand include a nature journal and pen/pencil, hand lens, binoculars, a bug jar for capturing and releasing spiders and insects, a camera, a super-special treat for when you reach the top of something, a container for a special mushroom or pine cone, and even a favorite figurine or toy that your littles are currently enamored with so they interact with that tree stump up ahead. Wet wipes, toilet paper, and Ziploc bags are also recommended. First-timer? Join a hiking group like Hike it Baby to hike with your peers and learn the ropes.

While it may be handy for you to navigate to each trailhead using your smartphone, remember that many of these wilderness areas have spotty cell service. As a general safety practice for hiking with kids, always tell a third party where you are going and when you expect to be back, and remember to tell anyone who may need to get ahold of you while you're away that you're not certain of cell coverage in the area. On the trail itself, every lead adventurer will have his or her own comfort level with safety, and you'll determine when your children will need handholding or reminders to stay close in tricky terrain, around exposed edges, or near water.

It's a given in the diversity of climates in Texas that you can encounter adverse weather conditions arriving seemingly out of nowhere. In certain desert areas of the state, you'll want to be aware of flash floods and not go hiking if there is rain or thunderstorms in the forecast—we've indicated which trails have this precaution. If thunderstorms are predicted, often in the late-summer afternoons in the West Texas mountains, it's best to plan a hike for another day or start and finish early in the day. If you find yourself in a lightning storm, immediately seek lower ground and avoid bodies of water or large trees—a thick patch of shorter, same-sized trees is best.

Teaching awareness and common sense and fostering an attitude of "there's no bad weather, only the wrong clothing" in these situations will go a long way toward creating an adventurous and resilient child. Model this "love the unlovable" attitude by remaining upbeat and playful as lead adventurer and you'll be amazed at how quickly their attention will turn back to the trail and its wonders.

In Central and East Texas, you'll want to check for ticks after hiking—they can appear in any season. They especially favor shrubby, grassy areas. Ticks don't fly or jump—they attach to hikers who come into direct contact and then feed on the blood of you, your dog, or other mammals on the trail. Wear light-colored clothing so you can quickly spot-check. Consider treating clothing with 0.5% permethrin or 20-30% DEET (be sure to apply on your children, avoiding their eyes, noses, and mouths). Stick to the center of the trail and don't go off-trail.

Remove a deer (black-legged) tick like this one (the only one that can spread Lyme disease) with tweezers or a tick-removal tool as close to the skin as possible

Make full-body tick checks a part of your routine back at the car. Be sure to check under arms, behind knees and ears, and between toes. Shower or bath time at home provides a chance for another full-body check. If you find one, remove it with tweezers as close to the skin as possible. Don't handle it with your bare hands. Clean the area with antiseptic/soap and water and call your doctor.

It is quite rare but you may also come across a black bear (*Ursus americanus*) or a mountain lion (*Puma concolor*) in the Big Bend area—be sure to give them a wide berth, back away slowly, and make yourself appear large by lifting your hands above your head. Do not run. Texas also has its variety of snakes, including a few venomous like rattlesnakes, water moccasins, and coral and copperhead snakes. Be snake aware and always look on the ground. Avoid moving rocks around, as they like to stay cool under there. If anyone gets bitten, seek medical attention immediately.

Always check in with rangers to see if there have been any animal sightings and if there is anything specific to be aware of at that time of year on the trail.

NATURE JOURNALING

Wendy received her first nature journal in Sydney, Australia, on her first night as a National Geographic Fellow with a group of students and teachers from around the world. It was leather-bound and bursting with empty pages, just begging to be doodled and documented in. Catherine Hughes, retired head of the National Geographic KIDS Magazine education team, gently guided us with a few key maxims for nature journaling:

- **MAKE QUICK, MESSY FIELD NOTES** You can add details later when you have free time, like during the drive home. You don't have to be a great artist to sketch something you see.

- **SKETCH THE MAP OF THE ADVENTURE THAT DAY**

PERSONALIZE IT Did someone say something funny? What was the most unique thing that happened on the adventure?

USE IT LIKE A SCRAPBOOK Add a trail brochure or ticket to your journal to remember your adventure.

Consider picking out a small blank journal for kids to bring along in their adventure bags. At power-up stops, when you stop for lunch at the destination, on the ride home, or later that night, encourage your little adventurers to create drawings of things they saw, document their observations of trees or animals, and press leaves or flowers.

One of my favorite techniques is to take one flower, branch, or leaf and draw it from several different angles. Each time you rotate, you'll notice new details you didn't see before. Or, you can create interesting compositions by drawing and layering multiple stages of a plant like buds, fallen petals, and full blooms. Similarly, when I draw animals, I often blend their natural patterns into the textures that surround them. Feathers, wings, petals, and leaves play together to create dizzying but satisfying patterns. It's like a game of hide-and-seek to discover where one plant or animal ends and another begins.

—Maggie Enterrios, author of *Nature Observer: A Guided Journal*

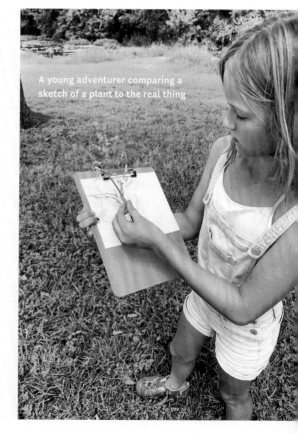
A young adventurer comparing a sketch of a plant to the real thing

DIGITAL CONNECTIONS

The social media accounts of many of the agencies that manage public lands in Texas are quite active, and they can be a great way for kids to use technology to enhance their experience in nature. They can ask pre- or post-adventure questions about conditions or flora and fauna, and the forums can be wonderful places to share images you snapped—for both you and your little adventurers. Search the location on Instagram for recent photos, and be sure to geotag yours to contribute to other hikers' searches as well.

After the hike, enhance and recap the experience by working with the kids on a trip report on one of these sites. Encourage them to define what really stood out to them about the experience.

- **ALLTRAILS.COM** This a crowd-sourced database of hikes built by a community of four million registered members that includes reviews and user-uploaded photos.

- **WILDFLOWERSEARCH.COM** This site has many good tools for identifying flowers. Some are as simple to use as uploading a photo and asking it to scan a database for you. It also has up-to-date lists of species in bloom.

- **INATURALIST.ORG AND SEEK BY INATURALIST** This Web- and app-based online community allows you to share your species observations with other naturalists around the world. It's also a great place to post a question if you can't identify something you found.

- **GEOCACHING.COM OR THE GEOCACHING APP** Geocaches are treasures hidden by other people with GPS coordinates posted online. If you're heading out on one of the adventures, check the website or app to see if anyone has hidden a treasure along the trail. If they have, use your phone to navigate to it, find it, exchange a treasure item or sign the log, and re-hide it where you found it.

HIKEITBABY.COM This online community promotes group hikes with other families. Kayla Klein, Director of Programs for Hike it Baby, continues the pitch: "Take the step! Get over it and get outside and find out what Hike it Baby's community is all about, like our No Hiker Left Behind philosophy. Everyone is there for the same thing—get babies outside. Go to Communities, find your localized community, and it will have a Facebook group there for your specific city. Many cities, like Austin and Houston, also have Ambassadors."

SMARTPHONES

You may have picked up this book to find ways of distracting kids from their phones and you already know where you stand on the issue of screen time. But if letting kids use a phone on the trail to take a photo of an interesting flower, navigate with a digital compass app, use the audio app to capture a birdsong, or share their photos of the hike on the state forest's Instagram on the drive home sounds like a conscientious way to bridge technology and outdoor time, go for it. Of course, not using a phone at all can be equally fun and appropriate.

Sara McCarty, founder of Run Wild My Child, has this advice for families: "Continue to encourage your kids to try new things, like hiking with you. You're never going to know what they're going to like or try. The reason kids want to be on screens is because of connection and socialization—get them outside with a friend and they'll be way more likely to stay outside." She also shares ways you can connect with other families by using the Run Wild My Child website to find new outdoor activities to try and to share your adventures on the #runwildmychild Instagram community.

SHOWING RESPECT FOR NATURE

Texas has 30 million lovely people, and enjoying and protecting its land will be key to conserving its beauty for generations to come. We are inspiring stewards—the more we are out there understanding and delighting in the natural world with our families, the more we and our little adventurers want to take care of it in the future. Some of the beautiful areas in this guide are also the most remote and precious. Please stay on the trail. You're doing the most important thing you can to keep the state beautiful: taking your kids outside.

You can't help but feel a part of something larger when you climb to the rim of Palo Duro Canyon or float in the clear waters of the Frio River. Simply by noticing and beginning to identify features, flora, and fauna in nature, you're creating a sense of respect and appreciation. Model and embrace the "Leave No Trace" ethos (see LNT.org for more great ideas) on each and every trail. Be diligent with snack wrappers and the flotsam and jetsam of everyone's adventure bag. Be sure to always stay on the trail and avoid trampling vegetation and disturbing wildlife to ensure that everyone and everything can share the adventure.

As young naturalists, the scavenger hunts will be asking kids to notice, to touch, and to play with nature around them in a safe and gentle way. For the most part, try not to take a leaf or flower off of a growing plant, but rather collect and play with items that are already on the ground. Manipulate them, stack them, create art with them, trace them in journals—but then leave them to be used by the other creatures on the trail, from the fungi decomposing a leaf to another kid walking down the trail tomorrow. Many of these wilderness areas and public lands were created with leaders in Texas, and you're creating the next generation of conservationists simply by getting them out in it.

A gentle reminder to stay on the trail

ADVENTURES IN WEST TEXAS / BIG BEND COUNTRY

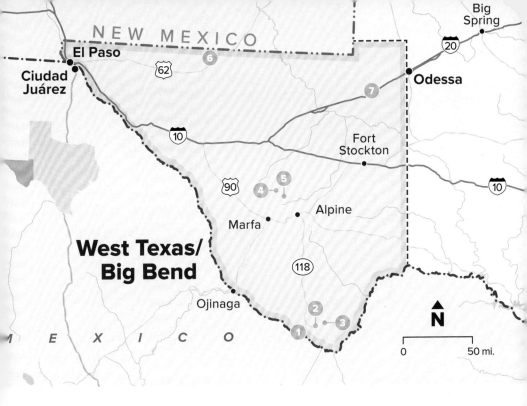

Adventurers, get ready to explore scenic canyons, windswept dunes, volcanic peaks, and big skies, because you have just arrived in West Texas. You'll begin with the crown jewel of Texas—the iconic Big Bend National Park, where you'll hike through the majestic Santa Elena Canyon, see an ancient dry waterfall, and loop around on top of the Chisos Mountains. The next West Texas adventure is 100 miles north of Big Bend in the Davis Mountains, which were formed by volcanic activity 25 to 30 million years ago. While you're in the area, you'll have a chance to explore the geological wonders of the Chihuahuan Desert, before heading 150 miles north to immerse yourself in the rugged beauty of Guadalupe Mountains National Park. Your final stop on this West Texas tour will be the enormous sandbox at Monahans Sandhills State Park. Bring a sled or rent one at the park and get ready for some dune sledding! Ready, adventurers? Embrace the Marfa motto, "Tough to get to, tougher to explain," and discover why this is such a special area of Texas. Let's go!

1

WALK THE RIM AT SANTA ELENA CANYON

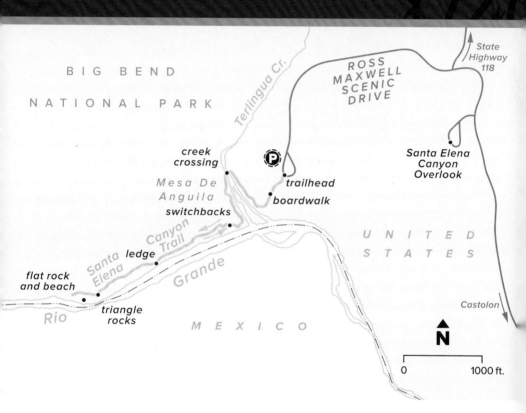

YOUR ADVENTURE

Adventurers, today you're going to see Mexico! You'll start off on the historical homelands of the Chisos, Mescalero Apache, and Comanche. From the parking lot, follow the boardwalk until you reach Terlingua Creek. For most of the year, Terlingua Creek is dry. But after a storm, it can reach your knees—call the ranger station to ask about conditions. Once you cross the

Take in the view at the mouth of Santa Elena Canyon at sunrise →

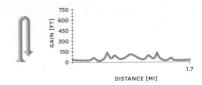

GAIN [FT]

750
600
450
300
150
0

1.7

DISTANCE [MI]

LENGTH 1.7 miles out and back

ELEVATION GAIN 148 ft.

HIKE + EXPLORE 2 hours

DIFFICULTY Challenging—Short, but has a steep exposed section of switchbacks with rocks; in some seasons you might need to wade the creek

SEASON Year-round, but extremely hot in summer; rangers caution to be off the trails by 11am and to stay hydrated. Fall and spring are best due to cooler temperatures, with wildflowers in spring months. The creek can flood, with danger of flash floods after a storm, so take precautions and check in at the visitor center.

GET THERE From the Panther Junction Visitor Center, take Gano Springs Road west 12 miles. Turn south on Ross Maxwell Scenic Drive for 21 miles, then continue onto Santa Elena Road for 9 miles—it ends at the parking lot.

Google Maps: bit.ly/timbersantaelena

RESTROOMS Yes

FEE $35 per vehicle, paid at the entrance station, or National Parks annual pass

TREAT YOURSELF Castolon has a small store where you can get ice cream treats.

Big Bend National Park
(432) 477-2251
Facebook @BigBendNPS

creek, you'll head up, up, up on several switchbacks—when you're at the top, take a picture of the view! Wave hello to the other side of the canyon—that's Mexico! After the switchbacks, follow the Rio Grande southwest, the trail traveling on some rocky terrain. Soon, it leads you to the riverside on the flat part of the trail. Keep going, past huge boulders. Take a few shore-side trails toward the river to touch the water and look down the canyon. Continue back along the trail through a maize hallway. You'll pass a huge overhanging boulder and finally reach the end of the trail at a beach, a perfect spot for powering up. Have lunch before turning back the way you came. Want more desert fun? Consider camping (in fall or spring) nearby.

SCAVENGER HUNT

Honey mesquite

Look for this shrub lining your walk up to the canyon. Feel its bright-green, feathery leaves. In spring, smell its yellow flowers. The best part of honey mesquite is its fruit, a brown, long pod hanging from the branches in summer. If you find a pod on the ground, pop it to help disperse the seeds!

Prosopis glandulosa bushes

Prickly pear cactus

This succulent (plants that hold water) puts on a show in early summer. Take a closer look at one plant. Count the pads and spines you spot. Are there tunas (red fruits)? How many?

Opuntia pads; *Optunia* flowers

Ocotillo

Look for this plant's tentacle-like branches reaching toward the sky as you climb up into the canyon. Each arm is called a stalk. Depending on the time of year, you might find them bare. In spring, they will be tipped with bright red-orange flowers. Other times, they're covered in small green leaves that appear after a rain. Sketch an ocotillo in your nature journal as you see it today.

Fouquieria splendens (*splendens* means "shining" in Latin, referring to the showy flowers)

Mexican palo verde

The bright, smooth green trunk of this deciduous (loses its leaves) tree looks almost like candy—its common name means "green stick" in Spanish. It has tiny leaves because the green trunk does the photosynthesis work, using light to change water and carbon dioxide in the atmosphere into energy and releasing oxygen. Take a big, deep breath and thank this plant for its oxygen today!

Parkinsonia aculeata plants; *Parkinsonia aculeata*'s itty-bitty leaves

Millipede

This insect is an arthropod, an animal with an exoskeleton, jointed legs, and no backbone. They love to come out after a rain. Each one has 160 legs, a pair of two legs per body segment. Can you do this math: If there are 160 legs, how many segments does a millipede have? Do you think the name "millipede" is accurate?

Diplopoda (means "two-footed" in Latin)

2

WALK THE WASH TO LOWER BURRO MESA POUROFF TRAIL

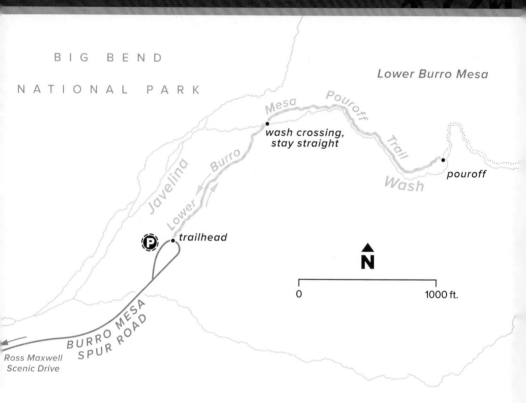

BIG BEND

NATIONAL PARK

Lower Burro Mesa

Mesa

Pouroff

wash crossing,
stay straight

Trail

pouroff

Wash

Javelina

Burro

Lower

Ⓟ · *trailhead*

▲
N

0 ——————————————— 1000 ft.

BURRO MESA
SPUR ROAD

*Ross Maxwell
Scenic Drive*

YOUR ADVENTURE

Adventurers, today you'll walk right into the heart of a canyon to see the effect water can have on rocks! You're on the historical homelands of the Chisos, Mescalero Apache, and Comanche. Above you is Lower Burro Mesa (a mesa is a flat-topped mountain). Begin your hike through a field of cacti. Soon you'll reach a wash (an area at the bottom of the canyon that's

Follow the trail into the wash →

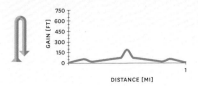

LENGTH 1 mile out and back

ELEVATION GAIN 200 ft.

HIKE + EXPLORE 1 hour

DIFFICULTY Easy—Flat gravel path that goes straight to the end of the canyon to see the dry waterfall

SEASON Year-round; gets hot in summer. Avoid when there's rain as it's prone to flash floods. Be sure to check the weather and with the ranger before heading out. The trail is exposed, so bring plenty of water and be mindful of sun exposure year-round. Spring and fall are best for cooler temperatures, and spring brings wildflowers.

GET THERE From the Panther Junction Visitor Center, take Gano Springs Road west 12 miles, then travel south on Ross Maxwell Scenic Drive for 11.6 miles. Turn right and follow the road for Lower Burro Pouroff Trail for 1.7 miles—the road ends at the parking lot.

Google Maps: bit.ly/timberlowerburro

RESTROOMS Closest are in Castolon

FEE $30 per car paid at entrance, or National Park annual pass

TREAT YOURSELF The historic Starlight Theatre in Terlingua, on your way out of the region, offers Frito pie, corn dog nuggets, and grilled cheese for a treat after your trek. Be sure to check out the ghost town and cemetery afterward.

Big Bend National Park
(432) 477-2251
Facebook @BigBendNPS

usually dry but can fill with water when it rains)—be sure to go straight here, as the wash continues for a while and looks pretty similar to your trail. The trail curves right and slowly starts to close in until you reach the very end. Look up at this huge pouroff—can you imagine water plunging out of here? Turn back the way you came; consider camping up at Chisos Basin when you're done, and be sure to get your stamp and Junior Ranger badge at the visitor center.

SCAVENGER HUNT

Lower Burro Mesa pouroff

This is a seasonal waterfall—during rainy periods, water flows through in a powerful flash flood and carves the rock and channel around you. It has stripes of yellow and orange ash-flow tuffs that are topped with rhyolite, an igneous (formed from lava) white rock. Feel the soil on the ground; because it's very dry and hard, it doesn't absorb water, allowing water to flow downhill—fast!

100-foot dry waterfall

Mexican buckeye

Look for this wash-loving shrub—you can spy its purple flowers in spring. The rest of the year, look for its big seedpods with three compartments. If you find one on the ground, dissect it and see if you can pry loose the three shiny black seeds inside.

Ungnadia speciosa; Ungnadia speciosa pods

Texas persimmon

This small evergreen (keeps its leaves) tree sprouts white flowers in spring and round black fruit in summer—see if you can count how many rounded-tip leaves it has on one stem. This species has separate male and female trees, so if you spot a fruit, you're looking at a female tree!

Diospyros texana

Cane cholla

Find this woody, skeleton-like succulent (holds water in its flesh) popping bright magenta flowers in spring, and afterwards, knobby yellow fruits. Look closely—how many segments of its "skeleton" can you count? Can you see how they overlap?

Cylindropuntia imbricata (*imbricata* means "overlapping" in Latin)

Desert willow

Look for the long, narrow, shaggy leaves of this deciduous (loses its leaves) shrub and its string bean–like pods. See if you can dissect a pod that's fallen to the ground, and sketch and label in your nature journal what you find. In spring, look for its best moment of the year—its beautiful pink and maroon flowers look like big bells jingling on the tree.

Chilopsis linearis

3

WIND YOUR WAY AROUND THE BASIN LOOP TRAIL

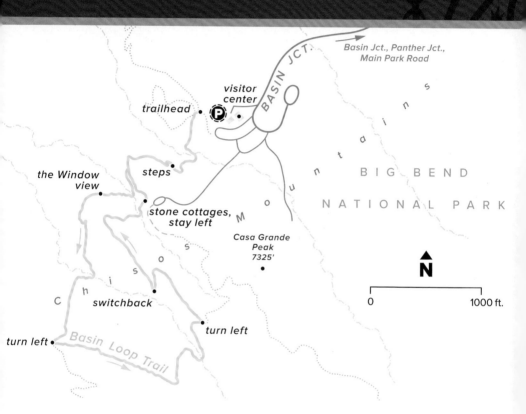

visitor center

trailhead

BASIN JCT.

Basin Jct., Panther Jct., Main Park Road

the Window view

steps

stone cottages, stay left

Casa Grande Peak 7325'

Chisos Mountains

BIG BEND

NATIONAL PARK

N

0   1000 ft.

switchback

turn left

turn left

Basin Loop Trail

YOUR ADVENTURE

Adventurers, today you're on the historical homelands of the Chisos and you'll be doing a loop with tons of views of the surrounding Chisos Mountains, the southernmost mountain range in the country. From the visitor center, find the gravelly, slightly rocky trail. It leads down to your

You're in the Chisos Mountains—the only mountain range to be completely contained inside a national park →

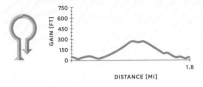

LENGTH 1.8-mile lollipop

ELEVATION GAIN 289 ft.

HIKE + EXPLORE 2 hours

DIFFICULTY Moderate—Fairly short with gradual elevation gain and rocky parts. Can be exposed; bring plenty of water and sun protection.

SEASON Year-round; fall brings great colors and cooler temperatures; spring is also cooler and has wildflowers. Summer temperatures are not as hot as the surrounding desert areas, but still warm and can bring thunderstorms and flash foods. In winter, it's a great place to take a break.

GET THERE From Panther Junction Visitor Center, take Gano Springs Road for 3 miles and turn south onto Basin Junction Road, which takes you 9 miles to its end at the Chisos Basin Visitor Center and the trailhead.

Google Maps: bit.ly/timberbasinloop

RESTROOMS At the parking lot

FEE $35 per vehicle, paid at the entrance station, or National Parks annual pass

TREAT YOURSELF Grab some food to go at the Chisos Mountain Lodge restaurant.

Big Bend National Park
(432) 477-2251
Facebook @BigBendNPS
Instagram @BigBendConservancy

first junction. Head right to take this route as a counterclockwise loop. The trail gradually starts to go up, offering amazing views, including the famous Window. Continue on to reach your second junction. Stay left here and continue along the trail until you reach another junction—with another left, the trail turns back and starts to close your loop. Soon you'll reach your original junction—turn right here and head back to the visitor center. Consider staying the night at one of the park's campgrounds or treat yourself and stay at the Chisos Mountain Lodge.

SCAVENGER HUNT

Carmen Mountains white-tailed deer

Let's be animal trackers today! Look carefully at the dirt and mud on the trail for twin sets of curved hooves. What does the pattern tell you about them? Were the deer walking or running? Which direction? Then look around you on the trail for their telltale white-rimmed tails or the antlers of the males.

Odocoileus virginianus subsp. *carminis*; The tracks can tell you a lot about an animal's behavior that day

Mexican pinyon pine

Watch for this bushy evergreen (doesn't lose its needles) dotting the trail today. Look closely—can you count its blue-green needles in bundles of three? These are called fascicles. Its cones are small and round—is the cone you find open, with its scales open and dispersing its seeds (pine nuts), or is it closed? Usually these cones open up in early fall.

Pinus cembroides

Black bear tracks

In the early 1900s, these mammals were common here, but by the time the park was established in 1944, they were virtually gone due to hunting, trapping, and loss of habitat. Amazingly, they began to return and can regularly be seen in Chisos Basin. The population is now believed to be between 30 and 40. Be sure to make plenty of noise on your hike; if you come across one, slowly back away, put your arms up to appear big, and do not run, which might provoke them to chase you.

Ursus americanus subsp. *eremicus;* Their paws have smaller pads in front than in back

Century plant

This evergreen succulent grows in a rosette (a circular cluster of foliage) and its leaves have spines on their edges. Once the plant is 20 to 50 years old, it will grow a giant stalk of yellow flowers that local bats pollinate. Even though it doesn't take quite a century (100 years) as its name implies, it takes a *looong* time for these plants to bloom, and they only do it once! What is something that you'll only do once in your lifetime?

Agave havardiana is the largest agave in the park

Brown-flowered hedgehog cactus

Look for these little succulent (holds water in its flesh) humps low on the ground—do their spines look like a hedgehog to you? Sketch one in your nature journal and give it a face like it's a cartoon! If you're visiting in spring, look for small, rusty-brown flowers blooming in the center and carefully give them a sniff.

Echinocereus viridiflorus (*echino* means "hedgehog")

4

MANEUVER THE MONTEZUMA QUAIL TRAIL

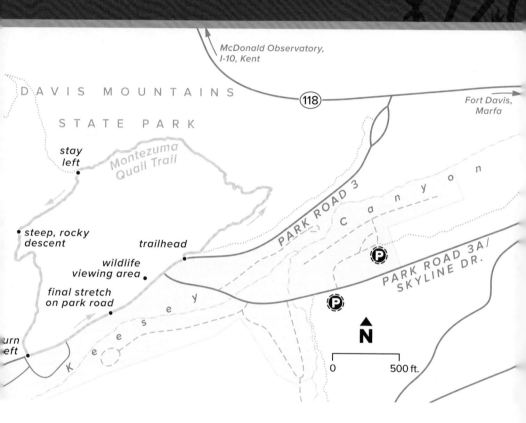

DAVIS MOUNTAINS

STATE PARK

Montezuma Quail Trail

stay left

McDonald Observatory, I-10, Kent

118

Fort Davis, Marfa

PARK ROAD 3

Canyon

PARK ROAD 3A / SKYLINE DR.

steep, rocky descent

trailhead

wildlife viewing area

final stretch on park road

Kersey

urn eft

N

0   500 ft.

YOUR ADVENTURE

Adventurers, today you'll be hiking on the historical homelands of the
Mescalero Apache and through Texas' most extensive mountain range.
Start at the Emory Oak Wildlife Viewing Area in the bird blind and see how
many birds you can spot. Then find the trail marker for the Montezuma
Quail Trail and get ready to climb! The first half of the hike will take you

This hike is nestled in the Davis Mountains →

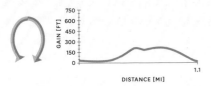

LENGTH 1.1-mile loop

ELEVATION GAIN 240 ft.

HIKE + EXPLORE 1 hour

DIFFICULTY Moderate—Short but rocky, with some elevation gain

SEASON Year-round. Due to the elevation, summers are slightly cooler here than in the rest of West Texas but still very hot. Bring plenty of water for summer hikes.

GET THERE From Fort Davis, head north a mile on Highway 17 to Highway 118 N, then west for 3 miles to get to the Park Road 3 entrance. This will take you to Davis Mountains State Park. From the park headquarters, head about 0.3 miles down the road to the Emory Oak Wildlife Viewing Area.

Google Maps: bit.ly/timberquailtrail

RESTROOMS Yes

FEE $6 for adults; free for children 12 and under; free with Texas State Parks annual pass. Be sure to reserve a day-use pass in advance.

TREAT YOURSELF Refuel with a grilled cheese sandwich or house-made dessert at the Black Bear Restaurant at Indian Lodge down the road from the wildlife viewing area and trailhead.

Davis Mountains State Park
(432) 426-3337
Facebook @DavisMountains
Instagram @DavisMountainsSP

to the top of a hill, where you can rest in a shady spot and enjoy the view. If you look closely, you can spot the McDonald Observatory in the distance. At the junction, follow the sign pointing you back to the campground. Prepare for a steep decline with some loose rocks—take your time and maybe try stepping sideways. At the bottom, there's a short walk along a very lightly trafficked road to get back to the wildlife viewing area where your hike began. Want to rest your legs but take in more views? Drive to the top of Skyline Drive for gorgeous views of the Davis Mountains during the day and for stargazing at night while you camp right in the park.

SCAVENGER HUNT

Rocky outcrops

Volcanic eruptions formed the Davis Mountains more than 25 million years ago, creating sheets of lava that cooled and hardened into igneous rock. Today the mountains consist of a jumble of peaks, ridges, and flatter areas scattered with rocky outcrops. Have you ever simulated a volcanic eruption at home using baking soda and vinegar?

A favorite habitat of the elusive Montezuma quail

Montezuma quail

This trail is named after a quiet, secretive bird called the Montezuma quail. It likes to make its home in the rocky outcrops you can spot while you hike. A Montezuma quail is usually less than 9 inches tall. What would your favorite hiding spots be if you were that little?

Cyrtonyx (means bent/curved in Greek for its claw)
montezumae (after the Aztec king)

Klein's pencil cactus

This succulent (saves water in its leaves) has spines that can easily attach to skin, fur, or clothing, so observe it from a distance. The long, hollow spines can also be used as needles. Have you ever tried sewing with a needle and thread? Look for its beautiful pink flowers in early summer.

Cylindropuntia kleiniae; The cactus's beautiful flower

Indian Lodge

As you near the halfway point of the hike, you'll be able to spot the Indian Lodge in the distance. The white adobe blocks were made from a mixture of water, straw, and soil. If you were going to build an outdoor fort or playhouse next to your home, what materials would you use? Write them down in your nature journal and make a sketch of your idea.

The Indian Lodge was built in the 1930s as an oasis in the desert

Silverleaf nightshade

This purple flower is most commonly seen from April to August. It has five petals that form a star shape. The leaves and fruit are poisonous to people and dogs, so make sure you don't ingest any and don't let your four-legged friends taste any part of the plant either. It grows about 3 feet tall, but the roots can go 6 feet deep into the earth!

This adaptation helps the plant find the water it needs to survive in very dry conditions. Do you know anyone who is 6 feet tall? Tell them they are as tall as a silverleaf nightshade's root system is deep!

Solanum elaeagnifolium

5

CHECK OUT THE CHIHUAHUAN SKY ISLAND

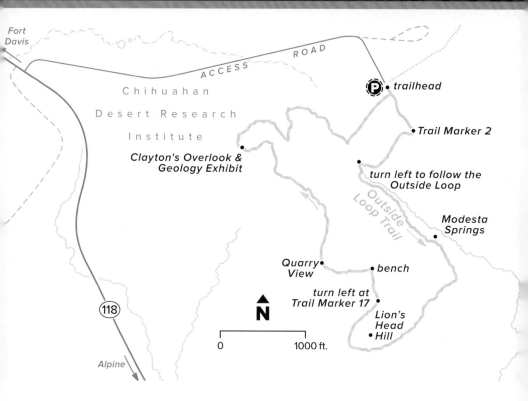

Fort
Davis

ACCESS ROAD

Chihuahan

Desert Research

Institute

Clayton's Overlook &
Geology Exhibit

trailhead

Trail Marker 2

turn left to follow the
Outside Loop

Outside
Loop Trail

Modesta
Springs

Quarry
View

bench

turn left at
Trail Marker 17

N

Lion's
Head
Hill

118

0   1000 ft.

Alpine

YOUR ADVENTURE

Adventurers, today you'll be going on a desert excursion through the largest
desert in North America and the historical homelands of the Jumano, Mescalero Apache, and Lipan Apache. It doesn't look like your typical desert
though; that's because it's a "sky island," an isolated range that pops up
from nowhere. Start behind the visitor center and follow trail markers for
the Outside Loop. At Trail Marker 2, take a sharp right to take the Outside

Explore the rock outcrops in the Chihuahuan Desert →

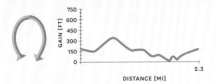

GAIN [FT]

750
600
450
300
150
0
2.3

DISTANCE [MI]

LENGTH 2.3-mile loop

ELEVATION GAIN 358 ft.

HIKE + EXPLORE 2.5 hours

DIFFICULTY Challenging—Rocky with a 200-foot descent into a canyon and a 200-foot ascent back up

SEASON Year-round. Monsoons arrive in July and August, cooling temperatures to daytime highs in the low 80s and turning the hills a beautiful emerald green.

GET THERE Take Highway 118, 4 miles southeast of Fort Davis, and turn left at signs for the Chihuahuan Desert Nature Center & Botanical Gardens. Parking is available at the visitor center.

Google Maps: bit.ly/timberchihuahuan

RESTROOMS Yes

FEE $6.50 for adults; free for children 12 and under

TREAT YOURSELF Enjoy an old-fashioned ice cream soda at the Fort Davis Drug Store Restaurant and Hotel or a Texas Tornado burrito at Lupita's Place, both located 5 miles up the road along Highway 118 in the Fort Davis downtown district.

Chihuahuan Desert Nature Center & Botanical Gardens
(432) 364-2499
Facebook @Chihuahuan-Desert-Research-Institute-31743057682
Instagram @CDRI_NatureCenter

Loop to Trail Marker 4—you'll take a left to start your 200-foot descent into the canyon, where you'll find Modesta Springs. Then, on your ascent, hike another 0.5 miles to walk along Lion's Head Hill—a huge mound of giant, upended rocks. Soon, you'll find a bench with a view, perfect for a power-up break. At Trail Marker 17 you'll find a green sign with a map. Turn left to continue to Quarry View and Clayton's Overlook (or right for a shortcut back to the trailhead). At Quarry View there's a range viewer that provides a close-up view of the rhyolite (volcanic rock formed from rapidly cooling magma) formations. Another 0.5 miles down the trail you'll come to Clayton's Overlook, with a geological exhibit of illustrations and descriptions of the mountains in view. Continue through the exhibit for a final 0.5 miles back to the visitor center, then make a final left to close out the loop.

SCAVENGER HUNT

Modesta Canyon

Notice the rocks on both sides of this canyon. The right side is made of intrusive igneous rock that cooled under the Earth's surface. On the left side, the canyon is made of huge boulders of extrusive igneous rock, which cooled on top of the Earth's surface. Look closely—what differences do you notice between the rocks on either side?

Where intrusive and extrusive igneous (volcanic) rock meet

Texas madrone

This deciduous (loses its leaves) tree is rare in Texas and has distinctive bark that peels off in sheets revealing smooth, red bark underneath. In spring, look for its sweet-smelling, bell-shaped flowers and the honeybees that love them. In fall, look for its red berries and the birds that eat them.

Arbutus ("strawberry" in Latin for its red berries) *xalapensis*

Orange crustose lichen

See the colorful spots on some of the rocks? These patches are lichens, and there are several species living in this desert. Not quite a plant, a lichen is a symbiotic combination of fungus and algae that gets its nutrients from the air and rain. There are three different types—crustose (like this one), foliose (leafy), and fruticose (stringy). How many different colors of lichens can you find?

Lichens come in a rich variety of colors

Sleeping Lion Formation

As you climb out of Modesta Canyon, you'll reach the end of the 15-mile-long Sleeping Lion Formation, which is made of rhyolite created by a lava flow and ash-flow tuff. Tuff is a light porous rock formed by consolidation of volcanic ash. The rock formation gets its name because lions often sleep close to each other, and from far away these rocks look like a jumble of paws, tails, and ears. Do they look like lions to you? Sketch what you see in your nature journal.

This rock formation was formed 35 to 37 million years ago out of molten rock, or lava

Mitre Peak

From the geological exhibit at Clayton's Overlook, spot Mitre Peak 6 miles away. It formed as a volcanic intrusion (under the Earth's surface) and is the remaining inside, or core, of the mountain. It's called a monadnock (a hill that rises out of flat land) or inselberg (German for "island" + "mountain"). Mitre Peak was named for a bishop's hat. Does it look like one to you?

Mitre Peak stands 6190 feet tall

RELAX AT TRANQUIL SMITH SPRING

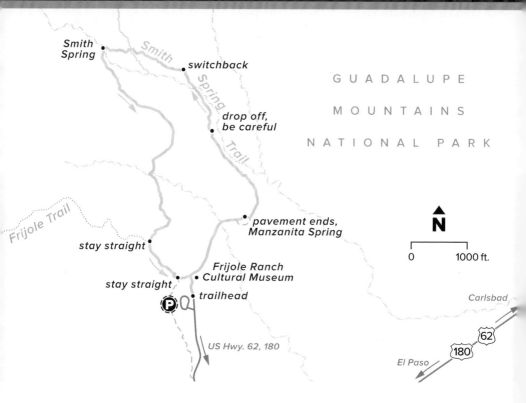

Smith Spring

Smith Spring Trail

switchback

drop off, be careful

GUADALUPE MOUNTAINS NATIONAL PARK

Frijole Trail

stay straight

pavement ends, Manzanita Spring

N

0   1000 ft.

Frijole Ranch Cultural Museum

stay straight

trailhead

P

US Hwy. 62, 180

Carlsbad

62

180

El Paso

YOUR ADVENTURE

Adventurers, today you're on the historical homelands of the Mescalero Apache and you'll be looping through the Guadalupe Mountains to a beautiful spring. Begin at the paved Smith Spring trailhead and head straight toward the Frijole Ranch House. Head a bit further—the pavement ends as you reach Manzanita Spring. Look for birds and animals here, then

Take in the rush of Fifth Falls! →

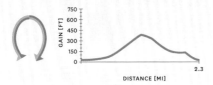

LENGTH 2.3-mile loop

ELEVATION GAIN 402 ft.

HIKE + EXPLORE 2 hours

DIFFICULTY Moderate—Some elevation gain and rocky terrain

SEASON Year-round. Spring and fall are the best times to visit, with fall bringing a dazzling color display.

GET THERE From El Paso, take US 62 E for 115 miles to Frijole Ranch Road; turn left and the parking lot will be at the end of the road in 0.3 miles.

Google Maps: bit.ly/timbersmithsprings

RESTROOMS At the parking lot

FEE $10 per person, payable via cash at the trailhead or credit at the Pine Springs Visitor Center, or National Parks annual pass

TREAT YOURSELF Snacks are just up the road at the Pine Springs Visitor Center.

Guadalupe Mountains National Park
(915) 828-3251
Facebook @Guadalupe.Mountains
Instagram @GuadalupeMountainsNPS

continue on your way. As you begin your climb, take your time and soak in the views. You'll pass a drop-off—be careful here. Soon you'll reach a switchback, pass some boulders, squeeze through another set of boulders, and arrive at a small pool and waterfall. Power up here—you're almost at Smith Spring! Take in the view on the bench, cross a creek, then the downhill begins. Squeeze between more boulders and after a while, you'll reach a fork with the Frijole Trail—stay straight here. You'll stay straight again past the Foothills Trail and find yourself back where you began. Turn right back toward the parking lot and consider camping at nearby Pine Springs Campground.

SCAVENGER HUNT

Soaptree yucca

Look for these sharp, long leaves in a round bundle on the ground on the trunk—in spring or summer, you may see a stalk shooting up from the middle to a height of 6 feet and adorned with white flowers. The leaves have silvery fibers that indigenous people harvested and wove, and its roots and trunks were used to make soap. Do you think you could weave something with these fibers?

Yucca elata (means "to lift up" in Latin)

Texas madrone

Look for these evergreen trees with dark green, taco-shaped leaves. Their bark is beautiful; it exfoliates (or peels) to reveal shiny orange beneath. Sketch winding shapes of these trees in your nature journal and add color when you get home to try to recreate the colors you saw.

Arbutus xalapensis bark; *Arbutus xalapensis* trees stand out in the landscape

Red-spotted toad

These amphibians love the rocky habitat you're hiking through today—be sure to go slowly and look carefully in crevices, because they use camouflage. The male's call sounds like a loud trill—try making that noise yourself now!

Anaxyrus punctatus

Javelina

These hoofed mammals can often be spotted crossing roads in south Texas and may be confused with pigs because of their snouts, but there are small differences. Javelinas have three toes on their hind feet while pigs have two; javelinas have short tails, while pigs

have long tails. They travel in groups of two to twenty-two called "squadrons"—what would you call the group you're hiking with today?

Collared peccary, *Pecari tajacu*, releases a strong musky odor when it gets excited!

Smith Spring

Look down at the ground—now imagine, deep underground, a reservoir of water collected in the permeable (allows water to pass through it) sandstone bubbling up to the surface. The animals around here come to the spring to get their fresh water. Do you see any tracks? Where do you get your water?

Relax like the animals who come to drink from this spring

7

WANDER THE WINDSWEPT DUNES AT MONAHANS SANDHILLS

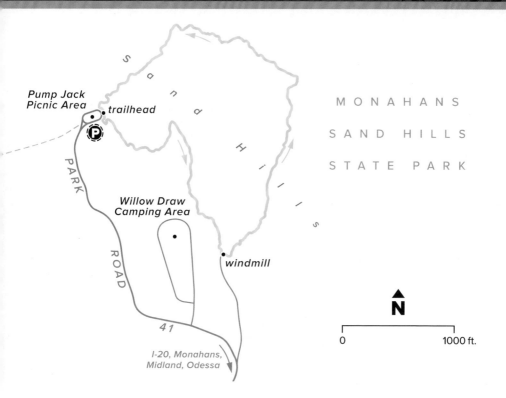

YOUR ADVENTURE

Adventurers, get ready to explore a Texas-sized sandbox! Today you'll be hiking on a dune field that extends 200 miles from West Texas into New Mexico, on the historical homelands of the Comanche, Mescalero Apache, and Lipan Apache. The dunes grow and change shape in response to the prevailing winds, so every day is a new adventure and there are no marked trails. There

Welcome to 3,800 acres of sandy fun! →

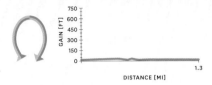

GET THERE From I-20, exit onto Park Road 41 to enter Monahans Sandhills State Park. Once you enter the park, drive east 2 miles to the Pump Jack Picnic Area to start your hike.

Google Maps: bit.ly/timberdunes

RESTROOMS Yes

FEE $4 for adults; free for children 12 and under, or with Texas State Parks annual pass. Be sure to reserve a day-use pass in advance.

TREAT YOURSELF Cool off with a snow cone at 12th & Snow in Monahans.

Monahans Sandhills State Park
(432) 557-3479
Facebook @MonahansSandhills

LENGTH 1.3-mile loop

ELEVATION GAIN 16 ft.

HIKE + EXPLORE 1.5 hours

DIFFICULTY Easy—No big elevation changes, but you have to walk through sand

SEASON Year-round, but the sand gets hot in summer. Fall offers cooler temperatures and calm winds. Be sure to reserve a day-use pass in advance.

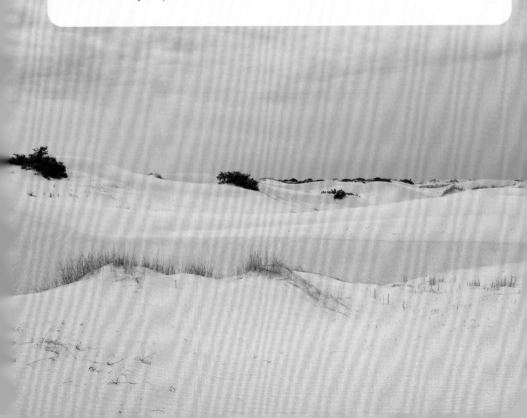

are two landmarks visible from the dune crests that will help you find your way—a windmill and a pump jack, which helps the piston pump in an oil well. To start your hike, find the Pump Jack Picnic Area. Climb to the top of the dunes and head right (southeast). You'll soon spot the windmill at the Sand-hills Picnic Area. Stay on the dune crests and walk to the windmill. When you get there, follow the dune crests around back to the pump jack. If you want to surf or sled on the dunes, stop by the visitor center to rent a round sand disk. Consider camping here to make it a weekend. Happy dune sledding!

SCAVENGER HUNT

Pump jack

Pump jacks are used by the petroleum industry to extract oil from oil wells and are a common sight in West Texas. This one is owned by the Occidental Permian company through a lease with the Sealy Smith Corporation. Long-term leases can be in place for many decades, often since before World War II. These leases originally prevented the National Park Service from acquiring the land needed to establish a national park in this area. In 1957, a state park was established instead, with land leased to the Texas Parks and Wildlife Department by the Sealy Smith Corporation.

These average 20 strokes a minute and can pump one to ten gallons of oil per stroke!

Historic windmill

The second landmark that will keep you on the trail is a historic windmill. Early settlers in the area found water by digging into the sand. Eventually, they built windmills to pump water up from deep below the shifting dunes. Speaking of water, take a sip from your water bottle to stay hydrated on the dunes!

Windmills like this one used to pump up water hidden beneath the dunes

Scaled quail

These bluish-gray birds are common in the park and eat seeds, leaves, and insects, mostly by pecking at the ground. You can find them foraging in groups called coveys, usually in the early morning or late afternoon. Groups will spread out across small areas, communicating by calling softly to each other. Like other quail that live in coveys, when scaled quail go to sleep at night, they gather in circular formations facing outward. Why do you think they do that? What position do you sleep in at night?

Callipepla squamata has a tufty white crest, hence the nickname "cottontop"

Mexican ground squirrels

These small rodents usually hibernate in winter and emerge in March or early April. Look for them hanging out in or near the park's shade shelters during the warmer months. They have a cool superpower—a natural resistance to the venom of diamondback rattlesnakes. Understanding how this resistance works can help scientists develop better treatments for snake bites. If you could pick a superpower, what would it be?

Ictidomys mexicanus has nine rows of white spots on its back

Shin oak

The green "shrubs" you see lining the dunes are actually deciduous (loses its leaves) oak trees that are only a few feet tall. Beneath the surface, though, they have enormous root systems that stretch as far as 70 feet, helping to stabilize the sand. The trees also provide a habitat and food for wildlife. Find their leaves and trace their toothy lobes in your nature journal. Search for their acorns in fall.

Quercus havardii on the dunes; Acorn of *Quercus havardii*

ADVENTURES IN
THE
PANHANDLE
PLAINS

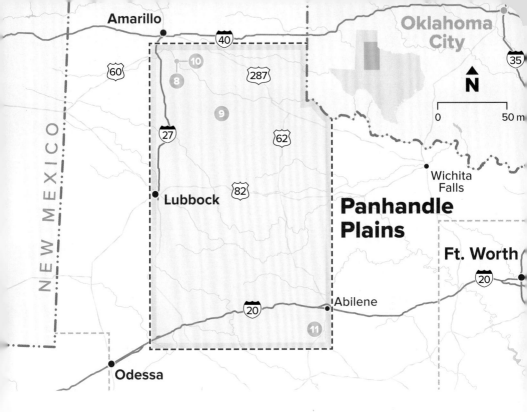

When artist Georgia O'Keeffe traveled to Palo Duro Canyon in the grassy Panhandle Plains, she described it as "a burning, seething cauldron, filled with dramatic light and color." Get ready to jump right into the cauldron because your first Panhandle Plains adventure takes you from the bottom of Palo Duro Canyon to the top and back. Don't forget to explore the Big Cave before you finish your tour of the second-largest canyon in the United States. Your next adventure takes you 90 miles southeast, to Caprock Canyons, home of the official Texas state bison herd. They wander freely around the park, so you may find yourself sharing a hiking trail or a road with a group. Always stay at least 50 yards away, drive friendly, and give them the right of way. The final adventure in this section of Texas takes you about four hours southeast to Abilene at Elm Creek. Here you will find a little slice of the Hill Country in the Panhandle, with shady oak groves, a creek to explore, and yurts for overnight glamping. Take in the Texas state motto—Friendship— and explore these trails with a hiking buddy. Let's go!

8

HIKE THE RIM AT PALO DURO CANYON

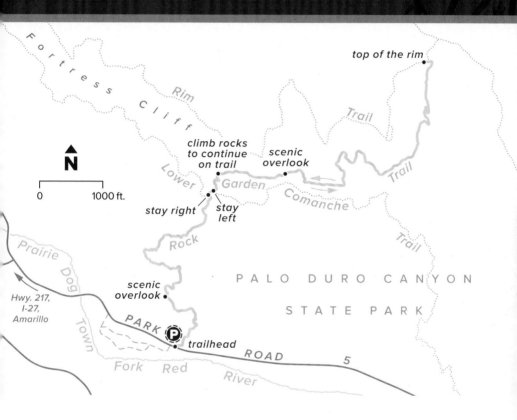

top of the rim

Fortress Cliff

Rim Trail

Trail

climb rocks
to continue
on trail

scenic
overlook

N

Lower

Garden

Trail

0   1000 ft.

Comanche

stay right

stay
left

Rock

Trail

Prairie Dog

scenic
overlook

PALO DURO CANYON

STATE PARK

Hwy. 217,
I-27,
Amarillo

Town

PARK

trailhead

ROAD

5

Fork   Red   River

YOUR ADVENTURE

Adventurers, today you'll be exploring the Grand Canyon of Texas. It has
been inhabited for about 12,000 years and is the historical homeland of the
Folsom and Clovis, who hunted mammoths and bison, and of the Apache,
Comanche, and Kiowa. You'll be hiking the Rock Garden Trail, which takes
you from the bottom of the canyon to the rim at the top and back down

Palo Duro is the second-largest canyon in the United States →

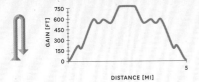

LENGTH 5 miles out and back

ELEVATION GAIN 777 ft.

HIKE + EXPLORE 3 hours

DIFFICULTY Challenging—Lots of elevation change as you climb from the bottom to the top, but worth the reward. Power up and bring plenty of water and sun protection.

SEASON Year-round.

GET THERE From Amarillo, take I-27 south to Highway 217, then go east 8 miles. The trailhead is nearly at the opposite end of the park from the entrance. The trail begins near the main road. There is a small parking lot across the road from the trailhead.

Google Maps: bit.ly/timberrockgarden

RESTROOMS At the Mesquite Camp area, a few minutes down the road

FEE $8 for adults; free for children 12 and under; free with Texas State Parks annual pass. Be sure to reserve a day-use pass in advance.

TREAT YOURSELF Grab some snacks or a cherry fried pie with ice cream at Buff's in nearby Canyon.

Palo Duro Canyon State Park
(806) 488-2227
Facebook @PaloDuroCanyonSP

again. You'll start in a field of boulders at the bottom. Heading up, you'll pass lots of unusual rock formations and scenic overlooks, so stop to take in the amazing views. About halfway up, the Rock Garden Trail meets the Lower Comanche Trail, merging for a few feet. Then stay on the Rock Garden Trail up the canyon, where you'll reach an especially rocky area. Carefully climb up the rocks to continue on the trail. After 2.5 miles, you'll reach the rim. Stop here, or continue for five minutes for more breathtaking views. See if you can tell just how huge this canyon is—120 miles long and 20 miles wide. In places, it is up to 800 feet deep! After a power-up stop and some photos, hike back down. Consider staying the night at one of the several campgrounds near the trailhead.

SCAVENGER HUNT

Palo Duro mouse

This rare small mammal inhabits the canyon walls at the park. Living in the steep, rocky terrain helps them hide from predators like coyotes, hawks, and owls, though rattlesnakes can still find and feast on them. Look around—can you find a place you'd try to hide if you were a mouse?

Peromyscus truei subsp. *comanche* has its largest colonies in Palo Duro Canyon and Caprock Canyons State Parks

Pedestal rocks

Shale and sandstone create unusually shaped pedestal rocks throughout the park. These rocks were formed by uneven erosion. Harder, erosion-resistant sandstone protected softer shale underneath. Pick a rock formation you like and sketch it in your nature journal.

Otherworldly sedimentary formations

Greater roadrunner

These birds can fly short distances of about 15 feet, but they prefer to travel on the ground, where they find most of their prey. They feed on scorpions, mice, lizards, and small snakes by running them down. The roadrunner is speedy—it can reach 15 to 20 miles per hour. That is close to the record speeds humans have hit (but only for about a mile)! Challenge your hiking buddy to a short race to see who is the roadrunner in the group.

Geococcyx (means "ground-dwelling cuckoo" in Latin) *californianus*

Texas horned lizard

This reptile is named for the four "horns" on its head that help protect it from predators. There are two large ones at the back and two small ones on each side. They are not made of bone like actual horns on other animals, but are instead specialized scales. If you had horns growing from your head, what would you do with them?

Phrynosoma (means "toad body" in Latin) *cornutum* ("horned")

Rock Garden

The first part of the trail winds through a rocky landscape of rocks, from pumpkin-sized ones to large boulders. Can you spot one that is about the size of you?

The trail gets its name from the garden of rocks of many different sizes

9

CAPER AROUND CAPROCK CANYONS

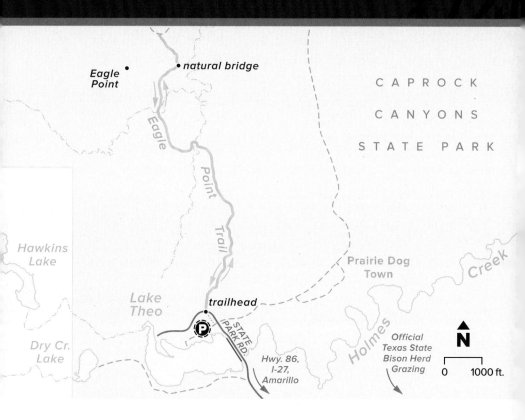

YOUR ADVENTURE

Adventurers, today you'll share your hiking grounds with a herd of bison! The official Texas State Bison Herd roams the plains of the park, which is also the historical homeland of the Folsom, Plains Apache, and Comanche. Starting near Lake Theo, follow the Eagle Point Trail. The trail is made of the red soil that the Panhandle Plains are known for. The first part will take

View from the trailhead of the Eagle Point Trail at Caprock Canyons State Park →

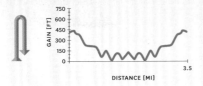

LENGTH 3.5 miles out and back

ELEVATION GAIN 449 ft.

HIKE + EXPLORE 2.5 hours

DIFFICULTY Challenging—A longer adventure with some elevation gain; exposed with no shade, so be sure to bring sun protection and plenty of water

SEASON Year-round. Spring and fall have milder temperatures. Spring is when bison calves are born and prairie dog pups emerge from their burrows. In summer, be sure to take plenty of water when hiking and avoid the hottest times of the day—summer temperatures can escalate into dangerous conditions.

GET THERE The entrance to the park is 3.5 miles north of Highway 86 in Quitaque on FM 1065. After stopping at the visitor center, follow the signs for a mile to park near Lake Theo for access to the Eagle Point trailhead.

Google Maps: bit.ly/timbercap

RESTROOMS At the nearby playground

FEE $5 for adults; free for children 12 and under; free with Texas State Parks annual pass

TREAT YOURSELF Grab a burger, fried okra, and a slice of cheesecake at Bison Cafe, a short drive away in Quitaque.

Caprock Canyons State Park & Trailway
(806) 455-1492
Facebook @Caprock.Canyons
Instagram @CaprockCanyonsStatePark

you down into the valley; about halfway through, you'll hike back up. About 2 miles into the hike, a little before reaching the turnaround point, you'll see a bench on the trail. This marks a "natural bridge," which creates a cave beneath the trail that you can climb through and explore. From here, you can continue just a little ways to the end of the trail or start your hike back the way you came. If you can stay the night at the Lake Theo Campground, you'll wake up to a spectacular view.

SCAVENGER HUNT

Bison

Bison usually roam peacefully through the plains, but park rangers recommend staying at least 50 yards away from them because they can be unpredictable. You may be able to tell a bison's mood from its tail. When the tail is down and swishing around, the bison is usually calm. When it stiffens its legs and body, it can mean that the bison is upset and ready to charge! Can you measure out 50 yards so you know how far to stay back?

Bison bison freely roam the park at Caprock Canyons

Black-tailed prairie dog

Along with bison, these mammals are a keystone species in this prairie ecosystem, meaning that other animals and plants depend on them. First, grazing bison create open spaces that attract the prairie dogs. The prairie dogs then settle in large groups called towns, creating a maze of inter-connected burrows underground. The tunnels benefit other animals like burrowing owls, ferrets, and foxes. When you're done with your hike, check out the prairie dog town at the Honey Flat section of the park.

Cynomys ludovicianus

Natural bridge

You're hiking along the Caprock Escarpment, a long, narrow rocky formation that separates the high, flat plains from the rolling ones to the east. If you take the small side trail down, you can explore this tunnel through the rock. Can you climb into the tunnel?

Erosion has carved a tunnel underneath the trail

Eagle Point

This 2733-foot peak was formed by the forces of 250 million years of wind and water. Can you see the layers—different colors, different textures, different thicknesses—in the rock?

Eagle Point dominates the view to the west on this hike

Gypsum

The red rock of Caprock Canyons is interlaced with white layers of gypsum. Gypsum is a soft mineral that measures a two on the Mohs Hardness Scale (the scale that measures the hardness of rocks—diamonds are at the top, measuring 10). Pick up some gypsum rock off the ground and try to scratch it with your nail. Does it feel soft or hard to you?

Gypsum layers in the red rock of the canyons

10

CLIMB UP TO THE BIG CAVE

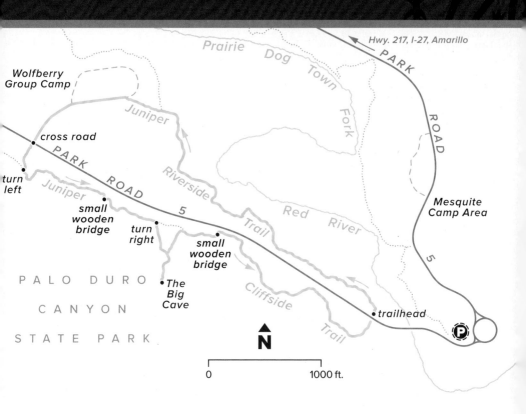

YOUR ADVENTURE

Adventurers, today you'll hike along red rock cliffsides and explore a cave as you trek the historical homelands of the Folsom and Clovis as well as the Apache, Comanche, and Kiowa. You'll start at the trailhead for the Juniper Riverside Trail. The trail parallels the Prairie Dog Town Fork of the Red River (which runs for 120 miles to the 1360-mile-long Red River) for about

The view from inside the Big Cave →

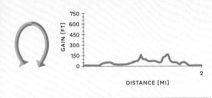

LENGTH 2-mile loop

ELEVATION GAIN 177 ft.

HIKE + EXPLORE 1.5 hours

DIFFICULTY Moderate—Mostly an
easy trail, but the rocky stretch leading
up to the Big Cave is challenging

SEASON Year-round.

GET THERE From Amarillo, take I-27 south to
Highway 217, and go east 8 miles. The trailhead
is nearly at the opposite end of the park from
the entrance. The trail begins off the main park
road. There is street parking by the trailhead.

Google Maps: bit.ly/timberjunipertrail

RESTROOMS At the Mesquite Camp
Area, a few minutes down the road

FEE $8 for adults; free for children 12 and
under; free with Texas State Parks annual pass.
Be sure to reserve a day-use pass in advance.

TREAT YOURSELF Enjoy a grilled cheese
sandwich or soda float at the Palo Duro
Trading Post inside the park.

Palo Duro Canyon State Park
(806) 488-2227
Facebook @PaloDuroCanyonSP

the first 0.5 miles. After parting ways with the river, you'll briefly walk along the Wolfberry Group Camp before crossing Park Road 5 and getting on a small hiking path that turns left to join the Juniper Cliffside Trail. After about 0.25 miles you'll cross a small wooden bridge. Shortly after that, you'll see the Big Cave in the cliffside up ahead. Power up here, then hike up to explore the cave! When you're done, turn right and cross one more wooden bridge on the final 0.5 mile stretch back to the trailhead. Consider making a weekend of it and camping at the Wolfberry Group Camp.

SCAVENGER HUNT

Spanish Skirts

Check out the colorful Spanish Skirts rock formations on the Juniper Riverside Trail. There are bands of red, white, and yellow rock layered throughout the rock formations. How many different layers of color can you see?

These were given their name by Spanish explorer Francisco Vázquez de Coronado

Wild turkey

Look for these birds or their tracks leading up to the water's edge on the Juniper River side of the trail. Wild turkeys have good eyesight during the day but cannot see well in the dark, so they usually roost in trees at night to stay safe from predators. If you were to spend the night outside, where would you sleep?

Meleagris gallopavo are usually most active early in the morning

Percolation caves

The sides of the cliffs on the Juniper Cliffside section of the trail have several percolation caves carved into them. The process starts with a small crack in the rock, and after millions of years it can expand to become an entire cave. Did you know that someone who studies caves is called a speleologist? Would you like to be a speleologist when you grow up?

Percolation caves were carved by moving water

American basketflower

When the basketflower is in bloom, you will see 4-inch flowerheads made up of hundreds of long, thin, pink-to-purple petals. This flower is a favorite of birds and butterflies. Birds enjoy the large, nutritious seeds it produces in late summer and early fall, and butterflies love the nectar. See if you can count how many petals are on a single flower.

Centaurea americana blooms from May to August

Big Cave

If you enter the cave, you will find a hole in the ceiling that gives you a small view of the sky. If you climb up around the outside of the cave, you can find that hole, and climb onto a top "shelf" on the canyon. Climbing around the back requires some fancy footwork and a grown-up to make sure everyone stays safe.

Climb up to Big Cave and explore the inside

11

HIKE THE SHADY BANKS OF ELM CREEK

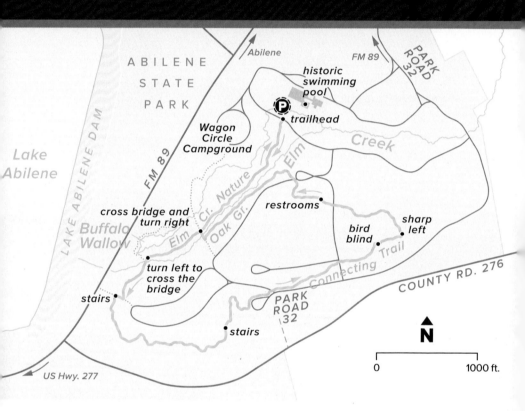

ABILENE
STATE
PARK

Abilene

FM 89

PARK ROAD 32

historic swimming pool

Wagon Circle Campground

trailhead

Creek

Elm

Lake Abilene

LAKE ABILENE DAM

FM 89

Cr. Nature

Oak Gr.

restrooms

bird blind

sharp left

cross bridge and turn right

Buffalo Wallow

Elm

turn left to cross the bridge

Connecting Trail

COUNTY RD. 276

stairs

stairs

PARK ROAD 32

N

US Hwy. 277

0   1000 ft.

YOUR ADVENTURE

Adventurers, today you'll be hiking through a grove of elm, oak, and pecan trees—an unusual sight in the plains of West Texas. This is the historical homeland of the Tonkawa and Comanche, who camped along Elm Creek while hunting bison. You'll start your hike today on the Elm Creek Nature Trail. After 0.25 miles, you'll pass a wooden bridge on your left then go

A bridge across Elm Creek →

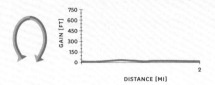

GAIN [FT]

750
600
450
300
150
0

DISTANCE [MI]

2

LENGTH 2-mile loop

ELEVATION GAIN 42 ft.

HIKE + EXPLORE 1 hour

DIFFICULTY Easy—Shady and flat

SEASON Year-round. Spring and fall migration seasons are the best times to see various bird species.

GET THERE From Abilene, travel southwest 16 miles through Buffalo Gap on FM 89, then continue on Park Road 32 to the park entrance. Follow the signs to the Elm Creek Nature Trail about 0.5 miles from the park entrance and just around the corner from the Civilian Conservation Corps (CCC) water tower and Abilene State Park Pool.

Google Maps: bit.ly/timberelmcreek

RESTROOMS Midway on the hike and at the nearby Wagon Circle Campground

FEE $5 for adults; free for children 12 and under; free with Texas State Parks annual pass. Be sure to reserve a day-use pass in advance, especially during peak seasons.

TREAT YOURSELF Enjoy an ice cream float at Blue Sky Texas, located about 12 miles up the road in Abilene.

Abilene State Park
(325) 572-3204
Facebook @AbileneStatePark

straight at the intersection with the Eagle Trail. Cross the wooden bridge over Elm Creek then climb a short staircase to stay on the trail. Hike another 0.25 miles, then take another staircase down. The Elm Creek Nature Trail ends at the paved circle. Turn right at the yield sign and take the short Connecting Trail on the left. Soon you'll pass a small cattle guard gate to join the Bird Blind Trail. Take a break and bird watch here! After that, the trail takes a sharp left. Continue on until you reach another camping area—the trail continues behind the restrooms. You'll rejoin the Oak Grove Trail for the last stretch of the hike. Cross the wooden bridge you passed at the beginning of your hike and turn right to return to the trailhead. There is a concession building and swimming pool nearby; if you're visiting in summer, cool off by taking a dip.

SCAVENGER HUNT

Mississippi kite

These white and gray hawks fly so gracefully that they appear to float, often gliding together. They look like acrobats, circling and swooping through the air as they feast on insects. Can you make gliding and swooping movements like them?

Ictinia mississippiensis is a small raptor with long, pointed wings

Painted bunting

These songbirds from the cardinal family are shy, but you may be able to spot them near a bird feeder at a wildlife viewing area or cautiously hopping along on the ground looking for seeds to eat. Male painted buntings are very colorful while the females are plain green. Do you have enough color pencils or markers with you to draw a pair in your nature journal?

A male *Passerina ciris*; A female *Passerina ciris*

Bird viewing area

These structures allow you to look at birds without them seeing *you*! Every season you can spot different birds through a blind—during spring, many are migrating from warmer areas, summer is a great nesting season for many species, hawks frequent the area in fall, and hummingbirds migrate. What season are you in, and which birds might you expect to see today?

Step inside and try to spot some wildlife

Elm Creek

The final Oak Grove section of the trail you take was built by the Civilian Conservation Corps (CCC) and follows Elm Creek. Plenty of wildlife use Elm Creek as a source of water so be sure to hang out by the water for at least five minutes and record anything you see or hear.

This creek feeds into Lake Abilene and provides a water source for many kinds of wildlife

Texas red oak

These deciduous (lose their leaves) trees have light gray, smooth bark. As they age on their way up to a lifespan of 200 years, the bark darkens and develops a heavier texture with grooves in it. How many lobes on the pointy leaves can you count? Collect as many acorns on the ground in 20 seconds as possible—how many did you get?

Quercus buckleyi produces vibrant red leaves in fall

ADVENTURES IN
HILL COUNTRY

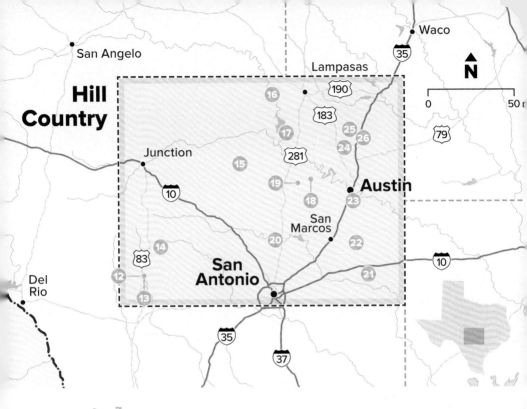

Adventurers, welcome to the Texas Hill Country! Get ready to explore sparkling rivers, limestone cliffs, cascading waterfalls, and rolling hills abloom with wildflowers. Begin your adventures about 90 minutes west of San Antonio, where spectacular views of green, rolling hills and clear blue waters await you after you summit Old Baldy at Garner State Park. In the same park, try a spelunking adventure at Crystal Cave. Travel about 40 minutes northeast to see a rock that looks like a monkey. Hop in the car again and continue 90 minutes northeast to visit Enchanted Rock State Natural Area, and summit a massive pink granite dome that has been a source of mystery for hundreds of years. Next, at the northern edge of the Hill Country, view a 70-foot waterfall and enjoy plenty of bouldering. Back towards Austin, visit a rocky canyon and a limestone moonscape with a waterfall along the way. Not far from north side of San Antonio, you'll have a river adventure before continuing to the Central Texas Tropics at Palmetto State Park south of Austin. Finally, you'll explore more waterfalls and rock formations. Pack your backpack, fill up your water bottle, and let's hop onto the trail!

12

SUMMIT OLD BALDY

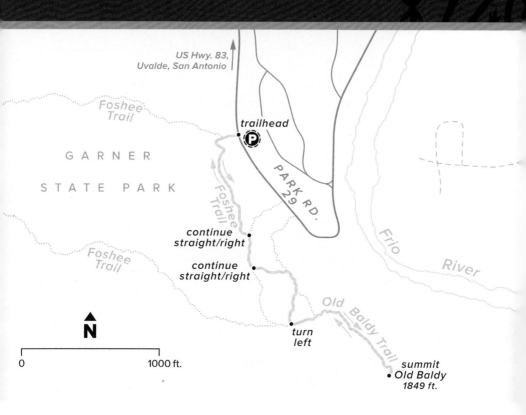

US Hwy. 83,
Uvalde, San Antonio

trailhead

Foshee
Trail

GARNER

STATE PARK

PARK RD. 29

Foshee
Trail

continue
straight/right

continue
straight/right

Foshee
Trail

Frio

River

Old Baldy Trail

turn
left

N

0   1000 ft.

summit
Old Baldy
1849 ft.

YOUR ADVENTURE

Adventurers, get ready for a big climb in the most popular state park in
Texas. Today you'll climb Old Baldy, on the historical homelands of the
Comanche and Apache. This short but challenging hike reaches its turnaround point at the top. There are no guardrails along the way or at the top,
so keep your littlest hikers close for safety. The hike begins with a gradual

The 1849-foot hill known as Old Baldy →

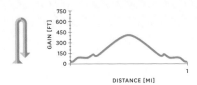

GAIN [FT]

DISTANCE [MI]

LENGTH 1 mile out and back

ELEVATION GAIN 439 ft.

HIKE + EXPLORE 1.5 hours

DIFFICULTY Challenging—Steep for little legs and rocky, but making it to the view is rewarding

SEASON Year-round.

GET THERE From Route 83, turn east on FM 1050 for 0.2 miles, then take Park Road 29 to the new entrance. Park by the restrooms

at the Pecan Grove Camping Area. The trailhead for Old Baldy is across the street.

Google Maps: bit.ly/timbermountoldbaldy

RESTROOMS At the nearby Pecan Grove Camping Area

FEE $8 for adults; free for children 12 and under; free with Texas State Parks annual pass. Be sure to reserve a day-use pass in advance, especially during peak seasons.

TREAT YOURSELF Grab some gelato or another frozen treat at the Garner Ice Cream Shop, located near the park pavilion.

Garner State Park
(830) 232-6132
Facebook @BrettAndTheDamReport
Instagram @GarnerStateParkTexas

ascent. Continue to follow the trail straight ahead, bypassing cutoffs to the left. After about 0.3 miles, you'll reach a T-intersection that takes you left towards Old Baldy or right for the Foshee Trail. Turn left to start climbing up Old Baldy. Most elevation gain comes from the last stretch, so take some breaks along the way. You'll see beautiful views of the Frio River. Once at the top, enjoy the amazing 360-degree views. If you're ready for another hike, check out Crystal Cave! When you're done, relax by the river at the Pecan Grove or Oakmont Camping Areas.

SCAVENGER HUNT

Crevice spiny lizard

This shy reptile (cold-blooded) likes to inhabit limestone rocks, where there are lots of crevices and cracks to flee into if approached. Most of the rock at this park is made of limestone, which is a porous sedimentary rock that allows water to flow through and dissolve the stone, leaving cracks, crevices, and sometimes even caves. Imagine if you were a lizard and look for spots in the limestone where you could hide.

Sceloporus poinsettii

Black-capped vireo

This small songbird gets its name from the black feathers on its head that make it look like it's wearing a black cap. It nests from about April through August. After that, black-capped vireos take off to the west coast of Mexico for fall and winter. If you could spend winter anywhere, where would it be?

Vireo atricapilla

Axis deer

Axis deer are native to India but were introduced to Texas in the 1930s and now compete with the native white-tailed deer for food. Garner State Park is home to about 200 of them. Like other types of deer, they are usually most active during the dawn and dusk hours. Are you usually awake when the sun is rising?

Axis axis

Frio River

Once you are about halfway up Old Baldy, you will be able to catch a great view of the Frio River. *Frío* means "cold" in Spanish, and refers to the cool, spring-fed water of the river. When you are done hiking, consider taking a dip!

The 200-mile-long Frio River winds through the Texas Hill Country

Old Baldy summit

Old Baldy and the other rock formations consist of two layers. The Glen Rose layer was formed over 100 million years ago, when dinosaurs roamed this area and left their footprints in the sand along the shifting margins of the ancient sea that covered Texas. The Edwards layer was

created on top of the Glen Rose layer, as the sea deposited additional porous layers of limestone. The beautiful views you see today are the result of the Edwards limestone uplifting about 65 million years ago, creating the dramatic, steep canyon walls around you. Sketch the layers in your notebook.

Give your fellow hikers a high five when you reach the summit

13

SPELUNK INSIDE CRYSTAL CAVE

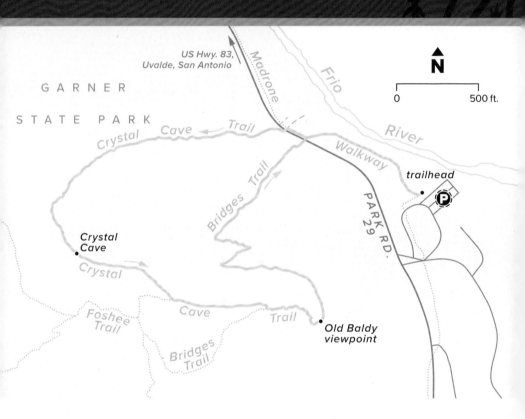

GARNER
STATE PARK

US Hwy. 83,
Uvalde, San Antonio

N

0   500 ft.

Madrone

Frio

River

Crystal Cave Trail

Walkway

trailhead

P

PARK RD. 29

Bridges Trail

Crystal
Cave

Crystal

Cave Trail

Foshee
Trail

Bridges
Trail

Old Baldy
viewpoint

YOUR ADVENTURE

Adventurers, get your flashlights ready because today you'll be spelunking
(exploring in a cave)! You'll start this hike on the historical homelands of
the Comanche and Apache with a short walk along the Madrone Walkway,
continuing right when it intersects the Bridges Trail. At the end of the
Madrone Walkway, you'll cross Park Road 29 to reach the trailhead of the

The view looking out from the entrance of Crystal Cave →

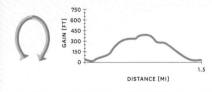

GAIN [FT]

750
600
450
300
150
0
1.5

DISTANCE [MI]

LENGTH 1.5-mile loop

ELEVATION GAIN 403 ft.

HIKE + EXPLORE 1.5 hours

DIFFICULTY Challenging—Short but steep and rocky in spots, so bring your best shoes and plenty of water

SEASON Year-round.

GET THERE From Highway 83, turn east on FM 1050. Go 0.2 miles to Park Road 29 for the new entrance. Park at the Garner Gift Shop. The trailhead is near the park pavilion.

Google Maps: bit.ly/timbercrystalcave

RESTROOMS At the nearby Pecan Grove and Oakmont Camping Areas

FEE $8 for adults; free for children 12 and under; free with Texas State Parks annual pass. Be sure to reserve a day-use pass in advance, especially during peak seasons.

TREAT YOURSELF Grab some gelato or another frozen treat at the Garner Ice Cream Shop, located near the park pavilion.

Garner State Park
(830) 232-6132
Facebook @BrettAndTheDamReport
Instagram @GarnerStateParkTexas

Crystal Cave Trail. After about 0.5 miles on that trail, start looking out for the cave, located on the right side. Once you find the entrance to the cave, get your flashlight out and explore. The cave is about 30 feet deep. Notice how the temperature drops dramatically as you enter. Once inside, shine your flashlight at the ceiling and you'll see where Crystal Cave gets its name. Once you exit the cave, you're close to the highest point of this hike. It's mostly downhill from here as you continue your loop. When you have about 0.5 miles left, the Crystal Cave Trail will merge with the Bridges Trail. Stay straight to reach the switchbacks on your way back to your starting point. Consider camping nearby at the Pecan Grove or Oakmont Camping Areas.

SCAVENGER HUNT

Texas madrone

The pavilion is connected to the Crystal Cave Trail by the Madrone Walkway, named for the Texas madrones growing here. Not many trees can handle growing on rocky limestone slopes, but this is exactly where these thrive. They grow slowly, taking a century or more to reach their full height of 20 to 30 feet, about 3 inches of growth per year. If you were this tree, how tall would you be based on your age?

Arbutus oaxacana is a rare tree with intriguing bark

Cave crystals

The crystals you see are made of calcite. As fresh water passes through the stone, calcium is separated from the rock and carried suspended in the water. Eventually, the water runs out of stone to filter through; calcite is precipitated out and crystallizes. Bring a flashlight into the cave to get a closer look!

Crystal Cave gets its name from the glittering crystals on its ceiling

Rock squirrel

These rodents, sometimes called black rock squirrels, look a lot like their gray or fox squirrel counterparts, except that the fur on their head and front half of their back is black or dark brown. They make their homes in rocky areas and are also excellent tree climbers. Rock squirrels sometimes hibernate in winter. They are called facultative hibernators: They hibernate only when they get very cold or low on food. What other animals hibernate?

Otospermophilus variegatus is found in rocky areas of central and west Texas

Engelmann prickly pear

The red fruit (also called a "tuna") of this succulent (holds water) is edible! Wearing thick gloves and using tweezers or pliers, you can remove the sharp spines and slice one open. There are hard, inedible seeds inside, which also have to be removed. Then you can use the fruit in a recipe—like jelly or juice. Some say that it tastes like a cross between watermelon and bubble gum. Don't take one from this wild setting, but consider ordering prickly pear juice next time you see it on a menu!

Opuntia engelmannii has beautiful yellow flowers in spring

Pavilion and dance floor

Ever since construction of this dance floor and pavilion in 1941, nightly dances on summer evenings have been held here. If you're visiting in summer, cool off in the Frio River after your hike and then stick around for The Dance. What is your favorite kind of music to dance to?

"The Dance" takes place here every summer night from Memorial Day to Labor Day

14

MAKE YOUR WAY TO MONKEY ROCK AT LOST MAPLES

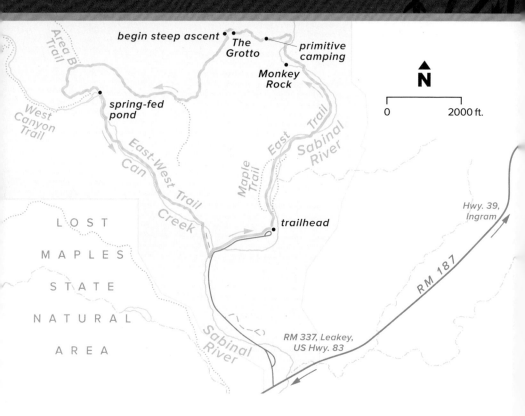

begin steep ascent • The Grotto • primitive camping

Monkey Rock

spring-fed pond

Area B Trail

West Canyon Trail

East-West Trail

Can Creek

Maple Trail

East Trail

Sabinal River

N

0   2000 ft.

LOST MAPLES STATE NATURAL AREA

trailhead

Sabinal River

RM 337, Leakey, US Hwy. 83

RM 187

Hwy. 39, Ingram

YOUR ADVENTURE

Adventurers, get ready for limestone canyons, clear springs, and a rock that looks like a monkey! If you're hiking in October or November, you may be in for a colorful fall foliage extravaganza. Your hike today takes place on the historical homelands of the Apache, Lipan Apache, and Comanche. Head right onto the East Trail to start your hike—the Maple Trail runs parallel, so

Monkey Rock is a highlight of this hike →

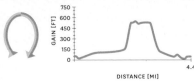

GAIN [FT]

750
600
450
300
150
0

4.4

DISTANCE [MI]

LENGTH 4.4-mile loop

ELEVATION GAIN 561 ft.

HIKE + EXPLORE 3 hours

DIFFICULTY Challenging—A longer adventure with a steep, rocky climb in the middle, but worth it for the cool rock formation

SEASON Year-round. Fall offers beautiful foliage. Spring boasts wildflowers and various bird species stopping on their way to their summer homes.

GET THERE The park is located 5 miles north of Vanderpool on Ranch Road 187. Park in the day-use area, past the headquarters and to the right. The parking lot is located 1.1 miles from the turn onto the park road from FM 187.

Google Maps: bit.ly/timberlostmaples

RESTROOMS At the parking lot

FEE $6 for adults; free for children 12 and under; free with Texas State Parks annual pass. Be sure to reserve a day-use pass in advance, especially during peak seasons.

TREAT YOURSELF Enjoy a slice of pie and hot beverage at Lost Maples Cafe in Utopia, 15 miles south of the park along FM 187.

Lost Maples State Natural Area
(830) 966-3413
Facebook @LostMaples

you can take that for the first stretch if you wish. It comes back to the East Trail after a short while. About a mile into the hike there's a small side path to the left—that's where you'll find Monkey Rock, a rock formation with an uncanny resemblance to a monkey. (If you reach a primitive camping area, you've just missed it.) Hop back on the trail and veer left after you cross over the Sabinal River. Pass the camping area and soon you'll reach the Grotto. It's easy to miss—look for a bench on the right side of the trail after a couple of creek crossings. Rest here, because you're about to begin a long, steep climb to the highest point on the trail. At the top, you can continue on your loop or turn left to a scenic overlook. On the East Trail, there will be two more overlooks on your left side. After the second one, go past both the Area B and West Canyon Trails. You'll soon emerge at a spring-fed pond that's home to channel catfish, winter trout, and the Guadalupe bass. Rest under the shade of the oaks—you're almost done! You'll merge onto the East-West Trail for the final mile of the hike and return to where you began. Perhaps camp overnight at a Lost Maples campsite!

SCAVENGER HUNT

Bigtooth maple

The name of the park, Lost Maples, refers to the deciduous (loses its leaves) bigtooth maples that are a relic from the last ice age (about 10,000 years ago). When ice sheets eventually retreated, scattered pockets of maples were left behind in the canyons of Central and West Texas. Today  these trees create Texas's best fall display—vibrant red, orange, yellow, and purple leaves. The show usually begins in late October and peaks in mid- to late November. Sketch an autumn maple leaf in your nature journal.

Acer saccharum subsp. *grandidentatum* ("big teeth" in Latin) has beautiful fall foliage

Monkey Rock

Thousands of years ago, water flowing through the Sabinal Canyon shaped this limestone into what now looks like a monkey. Do you agree? When you get home, use Play-Doh and try making your own Monkey Rock. Does it look like a monkey when you're done?

A limestone outcrop that looks like a monkey's face

The Grotto

It's easy to miss, but you will find it if you are on the lookout for a bench after getting back on the trail from Monkey Rock. Stand under the rock overhang during the warm months to enjoy some shade. Listen for the sound of falling water.

A former cave that has now opened up

Black maidenhair fern

These ferns like shady, moist environments. There are about 250 different kinds of maidenhair ferns. Black maidenhair has dark stems that have been used to make dyes. Have you ever made dyes or paints out of materials you found in nature?

Adiantum (means "not-wetting" in Greek) *capillus-veneris*

Texas brown tarantula

This arachnid (eight legs and no antennae) is a peaceful, nonvenomous spider, but it can bite when scared. Their abdomens also have small bristles, for ejecting into targets in self-defense. They aren't a threat to humans, so some people keep them as pets. Do you know anyone who has a pet spider?

Aphonopelma hentzi migrates and mates in summer

15

EMBARK ON A TRIP UP ENCHANTED ROCK

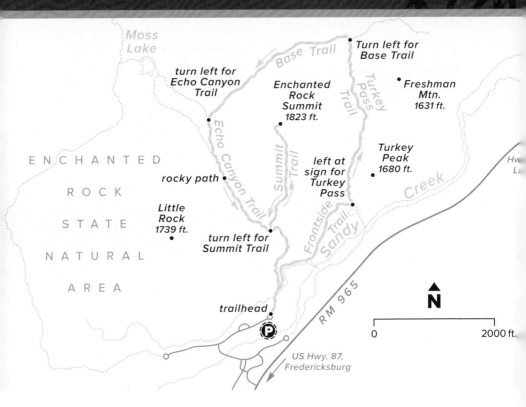

Moss Lake

Base Trail

Turn left for Base Trail

turn left for Echo Canyon Trail

Enchanted Rock Summit 1823 ft.

Turkey Pass Trail

Freshman Mtn. 1631 ft.

Echo Canyon Trail

rocky path

Summit Trail

left at sign for Turkey Pass

Turkey Peak 1680 ft.

ENCHANTED

ROCK

STATE

NATURAL

AREA

Little Rock 1739 ft.

turn left for Summit Trail

Frontside Trail

Sandy

Creek

Hw L.

trailhead

P

N

0   2000 ft.

RM 965

US Hwy. 87, Fredericksburg

YOUR ADVENTURE

Adventurers, today you'll ascend an ancient and mysterious 425-foot pink granite dome. It sits on the historical homelands of the Tonkawa, Lipan Apache, and Comanche. Begin at the Gazebo and take the Frontside Trail to your right, which runs for about 0.3 miles along the base of Enchanted Rock. At the sign for Turkey Pass Trail, turn left. You'll soon see Turkey Peak to

The view as you descend from Enchanted Rock →

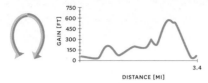

LENGTH 3.4-mile loop

ELEVATION GAIN 593 ft.

HIKE + EXPLORE 2.5 hours

DIFFICULTY Challenging—A steep climb up to the summit, plus some rocky areas

SEASON Year-round, but rangers strongly caution against hiking in July and August, when temperatures can get dangerously high. Fall and spring offer cooler temperatures and longer nights for stargazing at this International Dark Sky Park. Spring also offers wildflowers, birds, and butterflies.

GET THERE The park is 17 miles north of Fredericksburg on RM 965. From the park entrance, follow the road to the camping area then turn right. The trailhead is located 0.5 miles from the park entrance near the Gazebo at the end of the road.

Google Maps: bit.ly/timberenchantedrock

RESTROOMS Between the parking lot and trailhead

FEE $8 for adults; free for children 12 and under; free with Texas State Parks annual pass. Be sure to reserve a day-use pass in advance, especially during peak seasons.

TREAT YOURSELF Enjoy homemade fudge from Lone Star Candy Bar on Main Street in Fredericksburg, 17 miles down the road from the park.

Enchanted Rock State Natural Area
(830) 685-3636
Facebook @EnchantedRock
Instagram @EnchantedRockStateNaturalArea

your right. Continue for 0.6 miles, passing Freshman Mountain on your right. Turn left to join the Base Trail for a new view of Enchanted Rock. In another 0.6 miles, turn left again to join Echo Canyon Trail. You'll soon reach a rocky path that may require some fancy footwork to climb; help your littlest hikers. At the top, you'll be on flat ground for a short stretch before turning left and starting up the Summit Trail. This is the main event! Once you make it to the top of the 1823-foot summit, you'll get a breathtaking 360-degree view of the Texas Hill Country. Look for the small, geodetic survey marker at the top. This is a great place to enjoy your hard work and stop for a break. You'll turn left to join the main trail, then return to the Gazebo. Extend your adventure by staying overnight for great stargazing.

SCAVENGER HUNT

Turkey Peak

A billion years ago, there was a pool of magma (molten rock) hiding under the Earth's surface. Slowly, the magma pushed above the surface in some places, slowly cooling and turning into granite. These spots are the big rock formations you can see, including Turkey Peak. Does the surface look rugged or smooth to you?

Turkey Peak has an elevation of 1680 feet

Granite exfoliation

"Exfoliation" occurs with granite, formed deep within the Earth's crust. When the rock reaches the Earth's surface due to weathering or erosion of the overlying rocks, it releases the pressure on the granite and the rock expands slightly. This causes the rock to peel off in layers or sometimes as large boulders. Can you find a rock as tall as you are?

Granite rock peels off in layers or large pieces

Vernal pool

Vernal pools are formed when "weathering pits" at the top of the dome hold water for several weeks in spring. The pools develop into micro-habitats, or homes for specific groups of plants and animals, including tiny fairy shrimp. Trans-

lucent freshwater shrimp, they consume almost anything, from algae to microscopic creatures. There are no fish in these pools to act as their predators, but some birds will eat fairy shrimp. Vernal pools are an important part of the ecosystem, but the habitat is fragile. Without touching the water or disturbing them, can you spot any fairy shrimp today?

Vernal pools play an important role in the local ecosystem

Enchanted Rock

On cool nights following warm days, you may hear creaking noises from the contraction of the rock's outer surface as it cools. Hundreds of years ago, the Tonkawa attributed these sounds to spirits who enchanted the area. Do you hear anything today?

The big dome's back; View from the top, 25 feet above your starting point

Painted bunting

These birds love hanging out in the bush. How many different colors can you spot on the male painted bunting? Listen for the beautiful song—in spring, males like to sing up to ten songs to announce their territory! Try to whistle a bird song as you hike along!

Passerina ciris males are brightly colored

16

GAZE AT GORMAN FALLS

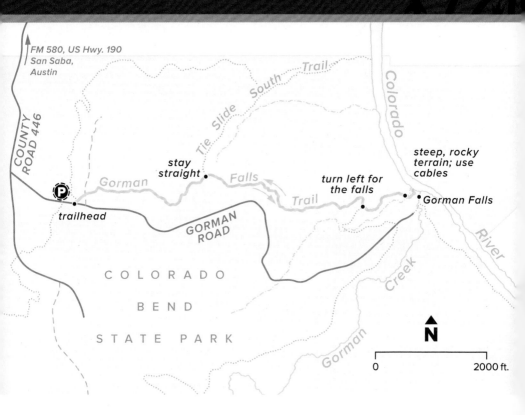

FM 580, US Hwy. 190
San Saba,
Austin

COUNTY ROAD 446

Tie Slide South Trail

Colorado

stay straight

Gorman Falls

Trail

turn left for the falls

steep, rocky terrain; use cables

Gorman Falls

River

trailhead

GORMAN ROAD

Creek

COLORADO

BEND

STATE PARK

Gorman

N

0   2000 ft.

YOUR ADVENTURE

Adventurers, today you'll hike to one of the biggest waterfalls in Texas, located on the historical homelands of the Tonkawa, Lipan Apache, and Comanche. You'll be exploring the Hill Country's unique karst (made from soft rock that erodes easily with water) formations. After taking Gorman Falls Trail for about 0.5 miles, you'll reach a fork with the Tie Slide trail.

Gorman Falls is a 70-foot high waterfall →

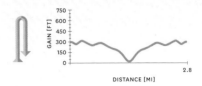

DISTANCE [MI]

LENGTH 2.8 miles out and back

ELEVATION GAIN 331 ft.

HIKE + EXPLORE 2 hours

DIFFICULTY Challenging—Mostly rocky and flat, but steep at the very end (use the cables provided for assistance and wear good hiking shoes); little to no shade, so wear hats and sunscreen and bring plenty of water

SEASON Year-round.

GET THERE From the intersection of Routes 281 and 183 in Lampasas, take FM 580 west 24 miles to Bend. When FM 580 ends at County Road 436, turn left and continue 0.3 miles before turning right onto County Road 440. Turn right onto County Road 442 after 0.5 miles. Take County Road 442 for 3.2 miles, then turn left onto Gorman Road. Soon you'll arrive at the parking lot—the trailhead is in the east corner.

Google Maps: bit.ly/timbergorman

RESTROOMS At the trailhead

FEE $5 for adults; free for children 12 and under; free with Texas State Parks annual pass. Be sure to reserve a day-use pass in advance, especially during peak seasons.

TREAT YOURSELF Grab some pizza or a burger at The Bend Cafe, 5 miles north of the park on CR 438.

Colorado Bend State Park
(325) 628-3240
Instagram @ColoradoBendStatePark

Stay straight until you reach Gorman Falls (you'll pass the Old Gorman Road Trail on your right shortly before reaching your destination). As you approach the falls you'll be able to hear the sound of rushing water. There's a steep, slippery section to descend before reaching the falls; make sure you hold onto the cables installed alongside the hill for safety. When you reach the waterfall, take a well-deserved break and enjoy the view before heading back up for the return hike. Make a weekend of it and camp right on the river at North Camping Area.

SCAVENGER HUNT

Horn coral fossils

The fossils embedded in the rocks on the trail leading to Gorman Falls are the bases of horn coral, creatures which have been extinct for over 250 million years! The fossil comes from the skeleton of the coral animal that lived inside a horn-shaped structure. The word fossil comes from the Latin word *fossus*, which means "having been dug up." Have you ever dug up a fossil? Sketch what you see in your nature journal.

Fossilized corals from the Paleozoic Era

Guadalupe bass

The Guadalupe bass is the official state fish of Texas; you won't find them in any other states. When baby fish are born, it's known as spawning and the babies are called fry. Guadalupe bass begin spawning in March and continue through April, May, and June. Do you know anyone whose birthday falls during one of these months?

Micropterus (means "small fin" in Greek) *treculii*

Colorado River

This 1450-mile-long river begins close to Lubbock and then flows southeast, going through Austin and many other cities before emptying into the ocean at the Gulf Coast. Have you ever seen another part of the Colorado River?

The Colorado River is the longest river that both begins and ends in Texas

Paleo-tufa

Leading up to and creating the foundation for the falls is a massive tufa deposit, covered with ferns and moss. Can you see the stalagmites (growing up) and stalactites (hanging down)? Some people have compared these formations to the architecture of Antoni Gaudí, who got much of his inspiration from nature. Do you think his famous cathedral looks like the tufa?

Tufa (sedimentary limestone rock) forms from an old spring outflow; One of Gaudí's buildings, the Sagrada Familia Cathedral in Barcelona, Spain

Gorman Falls

The highlight of this hike is the tallest continuously falling (year-round) waterfall in Texas. Unlike most waterfalls that shrink over time, Gorman Falls is growing. Mineral deposits gradually build up to form travertine rock, a type of limestone (which is made from the calcium of the bones of fossils!), causing the waterfall to get ever-taller. Think of the tallest person you know. How many of that person would it take to be as high as Gorman Falls?

Gorman Falls forms from Gorman Creek, which empties into the Colorado River

17

BOUND ALONG DEVIL'S BACKBONE

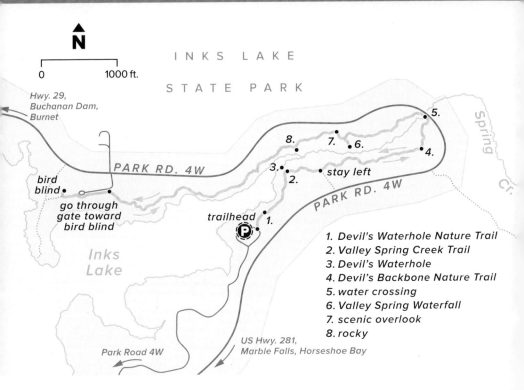

INKS LAKE

STATE PARK

Hwy. 29,
Buchanan Dam,
Burnet

Spring Cr.

PARK RD. 4W

5.

8. 7. 6.

3. 4.

2. stay left

bird
blind

go through
gate toward
bird blind

trailhead   1.

PARK RD. 4W

Inks
Lake

1. Devil's Waterhole Nature Trail
2. Valley Spring Creek Trail
3. Devil's Waterhole
4. Devil's Backbone Nature Trail
5. water crossing
6. Valley Spring Waterfall
7. scenic overlook
8. rocky

US Hwy. 281,
Marble Falls, Horseshoe Bay

Park Road 4W

YOUR ADVENTURE

Adventurers, today you'll walk across rocks that are over a billion years old on the historical homelands of the Apache and Comanche who first traversed this land. You'll begin on the Devil's Waterhole Nature Trail, which starts at the parking lot, crosses a small bridge, then ends at the Devil's Waterhole. Take a sharp right to join the Valley Spring Creek Trail. You'll

Cool blue waters below pink granite hills create a colorful Hill Country landscape →

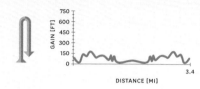

GAIN [FT]
750
600
450
300
150
0

DISTANCE [MI]
3.4

LENGTH 3.4 miles out and back

ELEVATION GAIN 190 ft.

HIKE + EXPLORE 2 hours

DIFFICULTY Moderate—A medium-sized adventure with some rocky sections

SEASON Year-round. Great swimming during summer.

GET THERE The park is located 9 miles west of Burnet. Take Highway 29 to Park Road 4. Drive south 3 miles to the park headquarters. From the headquarters, continue north on the park road for 0.8 miles, following the signs for Devil's Waterhole. There's a parking lot at the trailhead.

Google Maps: bit.ly/timberinks

RESTROOMS At the parking lot

FEE $7 for adults; free for children 12 and under; free with Texas State Parks annual pass. Be sure to reserve a day-use pass in advance, especially during peak seasons.

TREAT YOURSELF Grab some pad thai or a fried banana with ice cream at Aranya Thai Restaurant, 13 miles east in Burnet.

Inks Lake State Park
(512) 793-2223
Facebook
@InksLakeStateParkTexasParksAndWildlife
Instagram @InksLakeSP

climb up a hill now; after about 0.5 miles on Valley Spring Trail you'll merge with the Devil's Backbone Nature Trail. The trail makes a loose hairpin turn close to Park Road 4, at which point you'll have to cross a small creek. About 0.25 miles after the turn you'll see the Valley Spring Creek Waterfall down below. Hikers who want a challenge can climb down the rocks to check out the waterfall up close. Turn around and go left to continue on the trail. Soon you'll cross a tiny wooden bridge—you're almost at the Devil's Waterhole Scenic Overlook. There you'll find a bench with a beautiful view, so this is a great place to power up before you continue your hike along the north side of Inks Lake. The next part of the hike contains some rocky terrain. Follow the trail until you reach a gate—pass through it to reach the bird blind wildlife viewing area. This marks the turnaround point of the trail, so when your viewing is complete, hike back the same way you came. For added adventure, spend the night camping at Inks Lake State Park.

SCAVENGER HUNT

Devil's Waterhole

This deep swimming hole is surrounded by rock formations, with the largest rocks rising 40 feet out of the water. They called it Devil's Waterhole because settlers thought the devil was warming it up! Does the water feel warm today?

A popular swimming hole on warm days

Whitemouth dayflower

Dayflowers have blue petals, but this one gets its name from a bit of white in the middle. Each bloom lasts for only a single day, unfurling around sunrise but only open until midday. What are you usually up to during the hours between sunrise and noon?

Commelina erecta var. *erecta*

Gneiss rocks

This pink rock is Valley Spring gneiss, pronounced "nice." It is 1.3 billion years old. It was created so long ago that plants and animals weren't on Earth yet! The rocks were originally sedimentary and granite but became metamorphic gneiss rocks after millions of years of intense heat and pressure were applied. Gneiss is a hard rock, about the same hardness as steel! It's also a foliated rock, alternating layers of lighter and darker minerals. Look closely—can you see the layers?

This metamorphic rock juts up through the limestone in the park

Valley Spring Creek Waterfall

Valley Spring Creek Waterfall can be accessed from either side of the canyon, but it will take some maneuvering to get from the hiking trail down into the valley. The water flow depends on the season and rain level, but it's a beautiful spot to explore year-round. Is the water flowing today?

The creek flows into Inks Lake, man-made in the 1930s

Green-winged teal

You can find the green-winged teal in shallow water. They are dabbling ducks, tipping headfirst into the water to catch and eat insects, larvae, and aquatic plants. Only the females quack. Watch and listen for them near the water.

Anas (means "duck" in Latin) *crecca* has a gleaming green stripe on its head (males) and wings (males and females)

18

RUN AROUND REIMERS RANCH

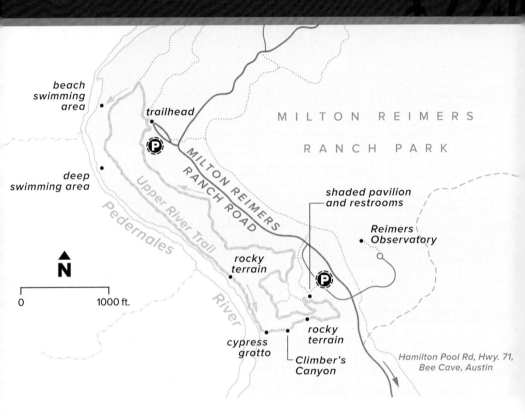

beach
swimming
area

trailhead

MILTON REIMERS

RANCH PARK

deep
swimming area

MILTON REIMERS RANCH ROAD

Upper River Trail

Pedernales

shaded pavilion
and restrooms

Reimers
Observatory

▲
N

rocky
terrain

0   1000 ft.

River

rocky
terrain

cypress
grotto

Climber's
Canyon

Hamilton Pool Rd, Hwy. 71,
Bee Cave, Austin

YOUR ADVENTURE

Adventurers, today you'll be visiting a park with world-class rock climbing
on the historical homelands of the Comanche, Lipan Apache, and Tonkawa.
Bring a picnic lunch and a swimsuit! Start by taking the trail in the far end
(northwest corner) of the River Trails Parking Lot. Take a left at the first
intersection, then head straight when you reach the river. It's shallow here

Reimers Ranch offers world-class rock climbing →

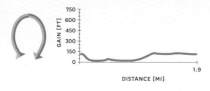

DISTANCE [MI]

LENGTH 1.9-mile loop

ELEVATION GAIN 144 ft.

HIKE + EXPLORE 1.5 hours

DIFFICULTY Moderate—A relatively flat trail with a steep section near Climber's Canyon

SEASON Year-round. Reimers Ranch does not take reservations (it's a large park and they do not expect to fill up or reach capacity).

GET THERE From Austin, take Highway 71 west. Turn left onto Hamilton Pool Road/ FM 3238 and follow the road for 12 miles. The entrance to Reimers Ranch will be on the right. After turning onto Milton Reimers Ranch Road, the River Trails Parking Lot is 2.3 miles from the entrance booth.

Google Maps: bit.ly/timberreimers

RESTROOMS Located in the River Trails Parking Lot and Pavilion Parking Lot

FEE Cash only—$5 for adults; $3 for anyone 62 and older; free for children 12 and under

TREAT YOURSELF Grab some barbecue or a snack at Jester King Brewery, 12 miles southeast of the park on the outskirts of Austin. The brewery is located on a working farm and dedicated to sustainability and conservation.

Travis County Parks, Milton Reimers Ranch Park (512) 264-1923
Facebook @Reimers-Ranch-Park
-172897852797346

(depending on rain levels) and perfect for wading. You'll soon come across sections of the river that are deeper and perfect for swimming. Continuing along the trail, you will traverse rocky terrain alongside some large boulders. Around the 0.75 mile mark, you'll follow the trail left to turn away from the river. Soon there's a beautiful area to the right with towering cypress trees and small waterfalls. Soak in the sights and sounds. Keep on and you'll reach a gorgeous band of limestone cliffs known as Climber's Canyon—a favorite spot for Central Texas rock climbers. The hike out of the canyon is steep and rocky, so prepare to help the littlest hikers on this part. Once you've made it up, it's less than 0.25 miles to a shaded pavilion with picnic tables and restrooms, a great place for a picnic lunch. From here, stay left and continue along the flat, granite trail on your way back to the trailhead.

SCAVENGER HUNT

Pedernales River

The Pedernales River is named for the Spanish word for "flint"; flint rocks abound in this area. It's a great place to cool off and enjoy the slow-moving current. Drop a leaf in and imagine it making its way all the way down to the Colorado River. You can find shallow areas with a beach-like entry and deeper places to swim, or just sit on a large rock near the bank and dip your feet into the water. Does the water feel warm or cold to you?

Over 100 miles long, this scenic river flows west to east across the Hill Country

Climber's Canyon

The park offers nearly 300 different climbing routes with varying levels of difficulty, from beginner to world class. Have you ever tried technical rock climbing?

Reimers Ranch is a favorite spot for Central Texas rock climbers

American beautyberry

Look for its white and pink leaves in summer and clusters of jewellike purple berries in late summer or early fall. The crushed leaves are a folk remedy used to repel insects. The berries provide food for wildlife and are also safe for humans to eat, though they're bitter. What is your favorite kind of berry?

Callicarpa (means "beautiful fruit" in Greek) *americana*

Chimney swift

These small, slender birds fly almost constantly, except when they are nesting or roosting overnight. They like to nest on vertical surfaces inside chimneys, as well as in enclosed hollow trees, caves, and wells. During migration season, you can find thousands of them roosting together in one spot. When they all funnel into a chimney together, the flock looks a bit like a tornado. Pretend you are a chimney swift and whooshing into an imaginary chimney!

Chaetura pelagica spends most of its time in the air

Agarita

Look for these mid-sized shrubs in small patches. Their sharp, leathery leaves deter deer from eating them, allowing the plants to provide cover for birds and small mammals. Look for the bright yellow flowers in late winter and pea-sized red fruits that follow in late spring. Carefully try to draw or trace the pointy leaf lobes in your nature journal.

Berberis trifoliata; The plant in flower

19

PLAY AT PEDERNALES FALLS

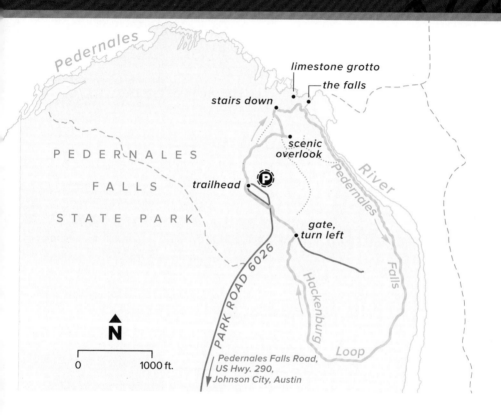

Pedernales

PEDERNALES

FALLS

STATE PARK

limestone grotto

the falls

stairs down

scenic overlook

trailhead

Pedernales River

gate, turn left

PARK ROAD 6026

Falls

Hackenburg

Loop

N

0   1000 ft.

Pedernales Falls Road,
US Hwy. 290,
Johnson City, Austin

YOUR ADVENTURE

Adventurers, today you'll be hiking along river limestone that is over
300 million years old. This land served as the historical homeland of the
Lipan Apache. You'll start at the Pedernales Falls Trail sign at the far end
of the parking lot and head down the hiking path that leads to the scenic
overlook of the falls. At the fork, take either trail to the scenic overlook. Once

A view of Pedernales Falls from the overlook on the trail →

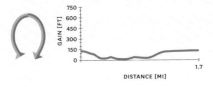

750
600
450
300
150
0

GAIN [FT]

1.7

DISTANCE [MI]

LENGTH 1.7-mile loop

ELEVATION GAIN 150 ft.

HIKE + EXPLORE 1 hour

DIFFICULTY Moderate—A shorter adventure with some rocky areas

SEASON Year-round. Spring is a beautiful time to see wildflowers.

GET THERE From Austin, take Highway 290 for 32 miles, then go north on FM 3232 for 6 miles.

Google Maps: bit.ly/timberpedernales

RESTROOMS At the trailhead

FEE $6 for adults; free for children 12 and under; free with Texas State Parks annual pass. Be sure to reserve a day-use pass in advance, especially during peak seasons.

TREAT YOURSELF Try a Mediterranean wrap or an organic hot dog at Lady Bird Lane Cafe, 12 miles west of the park along RM 2766.

Pedernales Falls State Park
(830) 868-7304
Facebook @PedernalesFalls
Instagram @PedernalesFallsStatePark

you reach it, descend the stairs to the river. You'll want to hike toward the right, following the river current, but take some time to explore the limestone moonscape and check out the falls. The limestone grotto is a short way upstream from the falls. You may need to use some fancy footwork to get through the tricky sections that are strewn with boulders and the tangly roots of bald cypress trees. After the river, you'll be on a solid dirt hiking trail. Near the end of the hike you'll reach a gate. Go through it and turn left to complete the loop and return to the trailhead. For an added adventure, spend the night at the Pedernales Falls Campground.

SCAVENGER HUNT

Pedernales Falls

On a beautiful, sunny day, the Pedernales River appears calm, but this can change quickly if rain arrives. In less than five minutes the placid river can turn into a raging flood. It's safe to explore here most of the time, but if it starts to rain, head toward higher ground. How would you describe the falls today? Peaceful picture or raging river?

Cascades over huge slabs of limestone, creating the falls; A grotto near them.

Bald cypress

These majestic wetland trees play an important role in bottomland (low-lying land by a river) forests. Bald cypresses are great at soaking up floodwaters and preventing erosion of the land. Raptors such as bald eagles and hawks nest in the treetops. Barred owls, wood ducks, and bees nest in their hollow trunks. The roots also provide spawning areas for bass fish. Examine one of these trees more closely. Can you find spots that would be useful for wildlife?

Taxodium distichum can reach up to 8 feet in diameter

Golden-cheeked warbler

This small, brightly colored endangered bird comes to Texas in March to nest and raise its young, then it leaves in July to spend winter in Central America. It uses long strips of shredded bark from Ashe juniper trees to build its nest. Do you like building nests or forts? What do you build them out of?

Dendroica chrysoparia

Redwhisker clammyweed

Redwhisker clammyweed—can you say the name of this plant five times fast? It gets its name from the clusters of long, red stamens (the pollen-producing parts of the flower) and the sticky residue that makes your hands feel clammy anywhere you touch the plant. Another unusual characteristic is its strong, rather unpleasant smell. If you are feeling brave, lean in a little closer and sniff the plant. What does it smell like to you?

Polanisia dodecandra

Rocky riverbeds

Find evidence of powerful flash floods nearly everywhere in this park. The floods can snap big cypress trees in half and move large boulders downriver and deposit them in new places. Many of the rocks are slightly different colors. How many different colors can you spot today?

Flash floods can carry massive boulders downstream

20

GO WITH THE FLOW AT THE GUADALUPE RIVER

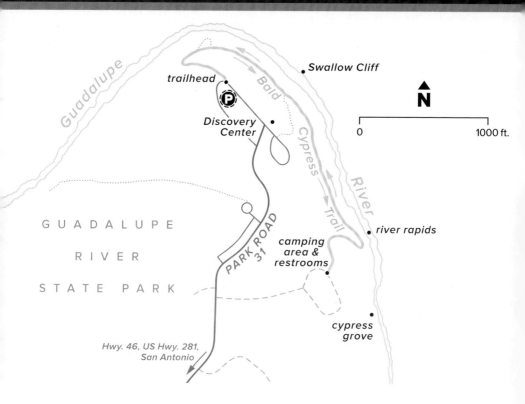

Guadalupe

Swallow Cliff

trailhead

Bald

Discovery Center

Cypress River Trail

N

0   1000 ft.

G U A D A L U P E

R I V E R

S T A T E   P A R K

PARK ROAD 31

river rapids

camping area & restrooms

cypress grove

Hwy. 46, US Hwy. 281, San Antonio

YOUR ADVENTURE

Adventurers, get ready to traipse through towering bald cypress trees and ride the clear rapids of the Guadalupe River on the historical homelands of the Tonkawa, Waco, and Karankawa. Stop at the park's Discovery Center, a hands-on nature center for families to explore, open on weekends from 10:00 a.m. to 4:00 p.m.. Check out Junior Ranger Explorer Packs with

Bring a tube and float down the Guadalupe River →

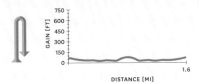

GAIN [FT]
750
600
450
300
150
0

DISTANCE [MI]
1.6

LENGTH 1.6 miles out and back

ELEVATION GAIN 95 ft.

HIKE + EXPLORE 1 hour

DIFFICULTY Easy—A shorter adventure with mostly flat terrain

SEASON Year-round; bring a swimsuit during summer to cool off.

GET THERE The park is located 30 miles north of San Antonio. Take Route 281 north and turn west onto Highway 46, then take a right (go north) onto Park Road 31. From the park entrance, continue 2 miles until the road dead-ends at a big parking lot near the river.

Google Maps: bit.ly/timberguadaluperiver

RESTROOMS At the parking lot

FEE $7 for adults; free for children 12 and under; free with Texas State Parks annual pass. Be sure to reserve a day-use pass in advance, especially during peak seasons.

TREAT YOURSELF Take Route 281 north for 20 minutes to grab a burger, salad, or grilled cheese at Beefy's on the Green in Spring Branch. There's outdoor seating with a play area out back.

Guadalupe River State Park
(830) 438-2656
Facebook @GuadalupeRiverStatePark

binoculars, magnifying glasses, sketchpads and more—free! Start your hike on the trailhead for the Bald Cypress Trail, which can be accessed from the leftmost side of the parking lot or by taking one of two sets of stairs on either side of the restrooms. You'll immediately see Swallow Cliff on the far side of the river. More than 240 species of birds have been spotted here, making this a designated Important Bird Area. The river is placid at the beginning of the hike, so it is a great place to wade or swim. After about 0.5 miles you'll come upon the picturesque rapids. Where the rapids begin, you'll start to see towering bald cypress trees with tangled roots along the riverbanks. Hiking here would be a serious obstacle course, which is why this root-filled section is not an official part of the trail. After the rapids, head back the way you came. If you need a restroom, there is one at the campground up the steep hill to the left. For an overnight adventure, book a campsite at the park.

SCAVENGER HUNT

Guadalupe River rapids

This is a popular spot to swim and play in the water in warm months. It's a good idea to check with a park ranger to ask if it's safe today. You can bring a tube or a float and let the current carry you through this stretch of the river. There are several spots with natural rapids as the river winds its way through the park.

The 250-mile-long Guadalupe River flows south into the Gulf of Mexico

Scissor-tailed flycatcher

Look for this bird with long and deeply forked tail feathers that give it its name. Mostly gray, scissor-tailed flycatchers have black wings and a salmon-pink belly. Its call is said to sound like a puppy playing with a squeaky toy. Do an impersonation of that and see if a bird comes out for you!

Tyrannus forficatus (Latin for "scissors") is a summer resident

Swallow Cliff

During nesting season, each pair of cliff swallows chooses a colony and picks a spot to build a nest. Each is built between a horizontal overhang and a vertical wall. Males and females both help build the nests by finding mud pellets, bringing them

back in their bills, and then molding them into place. Colonies can consist of 1000 nests. Have you ever made anything out of mud?

This cliff is home to a nesting colony of cliff swallows from spring to early summer

Ashe juniper

Ashe junipers are coniferous trees that keep their leaves and reproduce with cones. They grew here more than 100,000 years ago, when mammoths roamed the land. Mammoths were herbivores, so they may have feasted on the foliage and berries. Do you think it would be fun to be a scientist who studies prehistoric animals?

Juniperus ashei grows all over the Hill Country

Bald cypress

Have you heard of deciduous versus coniferous trees? Deciduous trees usually have leaves that change colors in fall and bloom with flowers in spring. Coniferous trees have needles instead of leaves and cones instead of flowers. Bald cypress trees are part of a special group that belongs to

both. They form cones, but they also change colors in fall and lose their needles. The "bald" in their name refers to the fact that they lose their needles early in the season. At this park, they usually change color around the end of October. Are there any needles on the trees right now? What color are they?

Taxodium distichum trees can adapt to a variety of soil types

21

TOUR THE CENTRAL TEXAS TROPICS

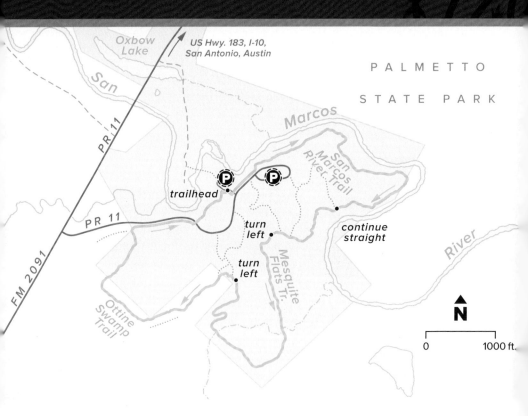

YOUR ADVENTURE

Adventurers, today you'll embark on a tropical hike through the historical homelands of the Tonkawa and Lipan Apache. Begin at the trailhead for the San Marcos River Trail and turn right toward the river. The trail is easy to follow and there are benches spaced about 0.75 miles apart along the way, perfect for power-up stops and snack breaks. At the next junction, the

Dwarf palmettos make this hike a botanical wonderland →

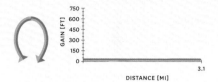

GAIN [FT]

750
600
450
300
150
0

DISTANCE [MI]

3.1

LENGTH 3.1-mile loop

ELEVATION GAIN 45 ft.

HIKE + EXPLORE 1.5 hours

DIFFICULTY Easy—A flat hike around the park

SEASON Year-round. Summer is great for playing in the river.

GET THERE From Luling, go southeast 6 miles on Route 183, then take Park Road 11 southwest for 2 miles. From the park entrance, follow the signs for the San Marcos River Trail. There is a parking lot at the trailhead.

Google Maps: bit.ly/timberpalmetto

RESTROOMS At the parking lot

FEE $3 for adults; free for children 12 and under; free with Texas State Parks annual pass

TREAT YOURSELF Enjoy an artisan espresso drink (for lead hikers) or an ice cream sundae at Mom's Front Porch, 10 miles northwest of the park along Route 183.

Palmetto State Park
(830) 672-3266
Facebook @palmettostatepark

Mossycup Spur Trail will be on your right—stay straight here, then pass the Canebrake Spur Trail, also on the right. About a mile into your hike, the San Marcos River Trail will meet up with the Mesquite Flats Trail—you'll take a left here. The trail continues for about another mile before merging with the Ottine Swamp Trail. Stay left at the merge. Palmetto-lined boardwalks take you over the park's swamps, making the Ottine Swamp Trail the most scenic of the trails you'll take today. On the final stretch of the hike, the trail intersects a road. Continue straight to finish the loop. For an added adventure, rent a one- or two-person kayak or stand-up paddleboard and explore the river after your hike. Campsites are available both near your parking spot and down the road at Oxbow Lake.

SCAVENGER HUNT

Dwarf palmetto

These evergreens (don't lose their leaves) are the park's namesake and create a tropical feel as you hike among them. Palmettos are more commonly found south and east of this area; in fact, this is the furthest west they are found. Dwarf palmettos grow less than an inch in height per year. How fast are you growing?

Sabal minor is one of 2500 plants in the palm family worldwide

Spanish moss

Spanish moss is neither Spanish nor a moss. It is a flowering "air plant" that gets its nutrition from the air and moisture from rain. Did you know it is called "grandpa's beard" in French Polynesia? If you can find some on the ground, hold it up close to your face. Does it look like a beard? Try it out, then pass it along so everyone can try on a "beard."

Tillandsia usneoides grows on large trees in tropical and subtropical climates

Cracked cap polypore

This hoof- or shelf-shaped fungus is saprobic, meaning that it gets its nutrients from decaying trees and logs. It helps decompose decaying organic matter back into the soil to be used by other plants and animals, making it part of nature's own recycling program. What types of things do you recycle at home?

Phellinus robiniae

San Marcos River

This river is home to several endangered species, including the fountain darter and the San Marcos gambusia (two small fish species) and the Texas blind salamander. These creatures thrive in clean water with a stable temperature. The San Marcos River provides the perfect habitat, with a 72-degree temperature year-round. Do you prefer to swim in warm or cool water?

This river starts in the springs of San Marcos and flows southeast for 75 miles before reaching the mouth of the Guadalupe River

Red-shouldered hawk

The red-shouldered hawk has black-and-white checkered wings, an orange-to-reddish chest, and a long, banded tail. These birds of prey are excellent hunters whose diets include snakes, lizards, frogs, fish, and crayfish, as well as small mammals like rabbits and rodents. They are diurnal, meaning that they are active during the day and sleep at night, like humans do. Their distinctive call sounds like a repeated "keeee-yer" sound. Can you try to sound like a hawk?

Buteo lineatus

22

LEAP AROUND THE LOCKHART LOOP

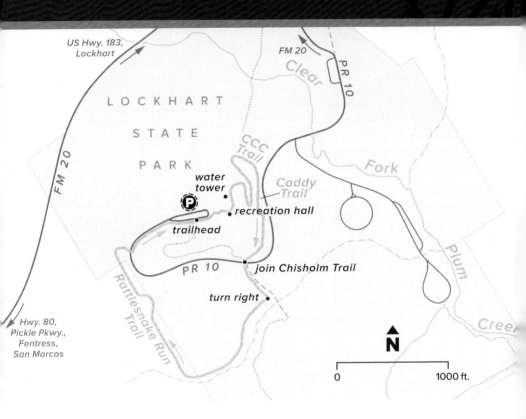

YOUR ADVENTURE

Adventurers, today you'll be exploring in the greenery of oak, elm, ash, and pecan trees on the historical homelands of the Lipan Apache and Tonkawa. Now a quiet getaway, life was not always so peaceful here. Just north of the park was the Battle of Plum Creek—a violent clash in 1840 between Comanche warriors and a Texas volunteer army which left over 80 Comanche dead.

Lockhart State Park is within easy driving distance of both Austin and San Antonio →

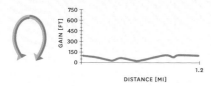

LENGTH 1.2-mile loop

ELEVATION GAIN 115 ft.

HIKE + EXPLORE 1 hour

DIFFICULTY Easy—Straightforward with minor elevation change

SEASON Year-round.

GET THERE From Route 183 in Lockhart, turn onto FM 20, then go southwest on FM 20 for 2 miles. After checking in at the park, continue along Park Road 10 for about a mile until it dead-ends in a parking lot near the Civilian Conservation Corps (CCC) recreation hall.

Google Maps: bit.ly/timberlockharthike

RESTROOMS At the headquarters and campground

FEE $3 for adults; free for children 12 and under; free with Texas State Parks annual pass

TREAT YOURSELF The Texas Legislature has proclaimed Lockhart the Barbecue Capital of Texas. Take State Park Road northeast to Main Street and grab some brisket or peach cobbler at Black's Barbecue, less than 3 miles from the park.

Lockhart State Park
(512) 389-8900
Facebook @LockhartStatePark

Begin at the parking lot near the scenic overlook, historic water tower, and recreation hall. From the back patio of the hall there's a pleasant hilltop view of nearby Lockhart. From the patio, take the steps that lead down the hill toward the golf course and Park Road 10. Before you reach the road, take a right to follow the Caddy Trail for 0.15 miles until it forks. Here, you'll take the Chisholm Trail by continuing straight at the fork, then immediately turn left and cross the park road. At a small creek crossing, turn right to join Rattlesnake Run Trail. Keep an eye out for the unusual trunks of the Hercules' club trees that dot the path. The last, short stretch of the hike is along the park road. For an added adventure, check out Lockhart State Park's family and children's activities, which include geocaching, fly fishing, archery, and more. You can also borrow fishing poles or get a Junior Ranger Explorer Pack, free of charge!

SCAVENGER HUNT

Civilian Conservation Corps water tower

The round structure you see peeking up from the top of the building was the original water cistern for the nearby CCC recreation hall. Later, the water tower's open-air structure was adapted to provide a gathering area for golfers waiting to tee off at the highest tee in Texas! Can you think of something else that the CCC built at a different park that you've visited?

The water tower was built by the CCC in the 1930s

Nine-banded armadillo

The armadillo is the state small mammal of Texas. Armadillos are born as identical quadruplets. The mothers give birth to four babies in March, either all female or all male. What would it be like to have three siblings who are identical to you?

Dasypus novemcinctus are cat-sized, insect-eating mammals

Hercules' club

In nature's pharmacy, there's Hercules' club: a tree with warty bark and thorns. All parts contain a chemical called xanthoxylin, which causes a numbing/tingling sensation when chewed. Native Americans and settlers chewed the bark and leaves as a toothache remedy (hence one of its names, "toothache tree"). Look for these along the Hilltop and Rattlesnake Run Trails. When you find one, make a sketch of the odd-looking trunk in your nature journal.

Zanthoxylum clava-herculis is easily recognized by the large, knobby warts on its trunk and branches

Maximilian sunflower

This flower makes its appearance in late summer to fall and is a great food source for animals. Caterpillars nibble the leaves. Butterflies and bees consume the nectar. Birds like to eat the seeds. Small mammals, including rabbits and ground-hogs, dine on the young plants, and larger animals like deer consume the older, taller plants. If you were an animal, would you prefer to be a caterpillar, butterfly, rabbit, or deer?

Helianthus (means "sun" in Latin) *maximiliani*

Western diamondback rattlesnake

Have you ever seen a snake flicking its tongue in the air? They use the tip of their tongue to bring scents from the air into a special organ at the roof of their mouth, which helps them interpret the informa-tion. On the other end of their long bodies you'll

find the rattle itself. If you hear the sound of the rattle, exit the area as quickly as possible without making any sudden movements. Their bite is venomous.

The rattle of *Crotalus atrox* is made of the protein keratin, the same protein your hair and fingernails are made of

23

LISTEN TO THE LOWER FALLS

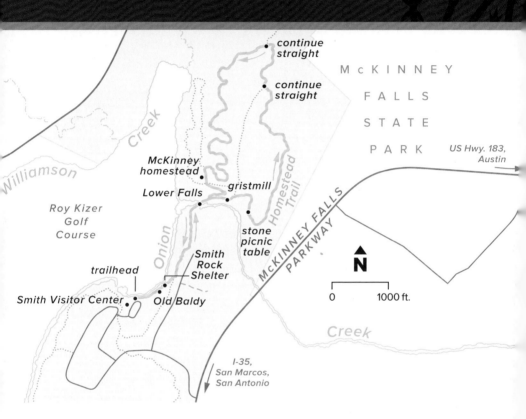

YOUR ADVENTURE

Adventurers, today you'll explore old shelters, landmarks, and a waterfall area on the historical homelands of the Tonkawa. Start your hike near the visitor center. Keep an eye out for Rusty, the resident red-shouldered hawk, often spotted flying around the area. Your first stretch is on the Rock Shelter Trail, where you will quickly run into the boardwalk bridge taking you around

One of two waterfalls at McKinney Falls State Park →

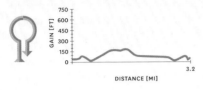

GAIN [FT]

DISTANCE [MI]

LENGTH 3.2-mile lollipop

ELEVATION GAIN 194 ft.

HIKE + EXPLORE 1.5 hours

DIFFICULTY Moderate—Mostly flat with a couple of water crossings

SEASON Year-round. Great swimming in summer. Early winter offers a tint of colorful foliage and a less-crowded park.

GET THERE The park is located 13 miles southeast of the state capitol in Austin off Route 183. Take McKinney Falls Parkway from Route 183 South straight to the park entrance. From the entrance, continue 0.7 miles and follow signs to the Upper Falls and Smith Visitors Center.

Google Maps: bit.ly/timbermckinney

RESTROOMS At the Upper Falls Parking Lot (always) and at the visitor center (Friday through Sunday, 9:00 a.m. to 4:00 p.m.)

FEE $6 for adults; free for children 12 and under; free with Texas State Parks annual pass. Be sure to reserve a day-use pass in advance, especially during peak seasons.

TREAT YOURSELF Enjoy creative flavors at Bésame Ice Cream just 4 miles north of the park in Austin. If you can't choose just one, try the tres besitos/triple sampler!

McKinney Falls State Park
(512) 243-1643
Facebook @McKinneyFalls
Instagram @McKinneyFallsStatePark

Old Baldy, a huge, 500-year-old cypress tree. Shortly after, you'll come upon the Smith Rock Shelter. Imagine what it would be like to live on the land and seek safety at night or during storms in a rock shelter like this. The shelter is named after the Smith family, who donated this land to the state in the 1970s. When you're done exploring the rock shelter, take a right and climb up a small ledge to merge with the wider Picnic Trail, then merge left for the Homestead Trail. When you see a vast limestone moonscape, you're near the waterfall— hear it? Near the waterfall, you'll cross Onion Creek to continue on the hiking trail. Stay right to go past the remains of an old gristmill on Gristmill Spur Trail and then continue straight on the Homestead Trail. Power up at the Smith family picnic table before winding through the Hill Country woods for about 2 miles. After about 0.75 miles, stay right to continue on the Homestead Trail, avoiding the shortcut trail to the left. In another 0.2 miles the trail will turn right for the Flint Trail. Keep straight on the Homestead Trail. From here, you'll hike the final 1.2 miles of the trail, ending your loop at the McKinney family homestead. The Homestead Trail continues to the right, but you can call it a day here. The homestead was built at the Onion Creek crossing of El Camino Real, a 400-year old, 2500-mile road connecting Mexico to Louisiana. Shortly after the homestead you'll cross Onion Creek again and pass the same sites to get back to the trailhead. For an added adventure, snag a campsite and spend the night!

SCAVENGER HUNT

Old Baldy

Old Baldy was sprouting here just as Leonardo da Vinci was painting the Mona Lisa! That means this tree has lived through a lot of changes in the world, from the harnessing of electricity to the invention of cars and computers. What new inventions do you think we will have 500 years from now?

A massive, 100-foot-tall, 500-year-old *Taxodium distichum*

Prehistoric rock shelter

The last known occupants here are believed to be the Tonkawa, with other groups using it from 6000 BCE until the eighteenth century. Would you make it your home in the park?

This limestone overhang is on the National Register of Historic Places

Lower Falls

The Lower Falls are created by Onion Creek flowing over a 15-foot limestone ledge into a pool below. This is one swimming hole at the park. The other is at the Upper Falls, but the water is deeper. If you don't want to swim, you can wade in up to your ankles or knees across from the falls.

The Lower Falls are a fun swimming spot in the warmer months

Gristmill ruins

A gristmill grinds grains like wheat or corn into flour using heavy stones. Millers had to watch the process closely to make sure the flour did not get too hot and catch on fire from the stones grinding together. For this, a sense of smell was important. Have you ever heard the phrase "keep your nose to the grindstone"?

The ruins of the McKinney family gristmill

McKinney homestead

Enslaved people built this homestead in 1850, and it was continuously occupied until it burned down in 1940. In 1873 the farm was sold to the Smith family, who farmed the land for several generations until they donated the land to Texas in 1973. What was life like for the people who worked on the land but who were not landowners?

The ruins of the home occupied by Thomas and Anna McKinney

24

MEANDER THE MEADOW AT GAREY PARK

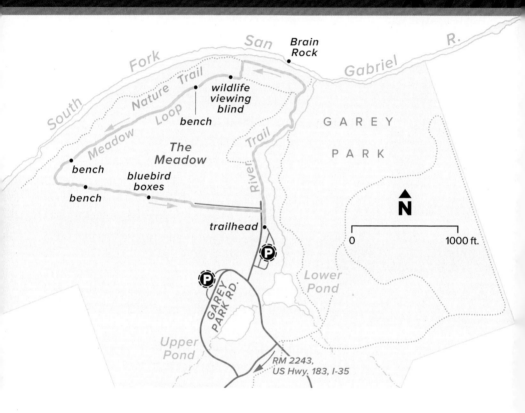

South Fork San Gabriel R.

Brain Rock

Nature Trail

wildlife viewing blind

bench

Loop

GAREY

Meadow

The Meadow

PARK

bench

bluebird boxes

River Trail

bench

N

trailhead

0   1000 ft.

P

P

Lower Pond

GAREY PARK RD.

Upper Pond

RM 2243, US Hwy. 183, I-35

YOUR ADVENTURE

Adventurers, today you'll be hiking along the South San Gabriel River in Garey Park, located on the historical homelands of the Tonkawa. From the trailhead near the A.M. Brown cabin chimney, you'll take the gravel Meadow Loop, staying right to head toward the river (you'll see a sign for river access). Stay straight the whole way, following the sign for the South

Explore the rock formations on the river at Garey Park →

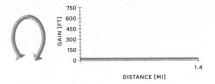

GAIN [FT]
750
600
450
300
150
0
1.4
DISTANCE [MI]

LENGTH 1.4-mile loop

ELEVATION GAIN 45 ft.

HIKE + EXPLORE 1 hour

DIFFICULTY Easy—An open and flat trail

SEASON Year-round.

GET THERE Garey Park is located approximately 6.5 miles west of I-35 on Leander Road (RM 2243). From the park entrance, continue straight for 1.1 miles, following the signs for Garey House. At the house, turn right into the large parking lot. The trailhead is on the other side of the pedestrian gate.

Google Maps: bit.ly/timbergareypark

RESTROOMS At the parking lot near the trailhead

FEE $4 per person; free for children 3 and under

TREAT YOURSELF Grab a taco, street corn, or fried cookie dough at Torchy's Tacos, about 7 miles south of the park on Whitestone Boulevard (FM 1431).

Garey Park
(512) 930-6800
Facebook @GareyParkGTX

Fork of the San Gabriel River. Power up on the bench. Head back just a bit and turn right to walk along the river on the Nature Trail, exploring huge rock formations in the river, including one that looks like a brain! When you're done exploring, walk uphill to rejoin the Meadow Loop near the wildlife viewing blind. There's a whiteboard inside the blind with a list of bird species that have recently been sighted. Can you spot any to add to the list? Once you're finished looking for wildlife, turn right to continue on the trail. Follow the Meadow Loop around the field, where you'll find more benches, and explore the 15 bluebird nesting boxes before returning to the trailhead. Be sure to check out the huge playground and splash pad at Garey Park before you leave.

SCAVENGER HUNT

Limestone rock formations

Millions of years of water streaming against rock have created these outcrops in the South San Gabriel River. This limestone formation has fossils dating back to the Cretaceous period, which means the rock is between 70 and 120 million years old. The large rock in the river is called Brain Rock. Does it look like a brain to you?

These rocks date back to the Cretaceous period, when dinosaurs roamed the land

Bluebird nesting boxes

In the park you can find 15 nesting bluebird boxes; in spring, you might see fledglings coming out and learning how to fly. Eastern bluebirds almost went extinct, but conservation efforts like the placement of bluebird boxes and backyard bird feeding have increased their numbers.

Nesting box; *Sialia sialis*

Plainbelly watersnake

This large, thick reptile ranges in color from black to brown to greenish gray with a yellow underbelly. It gets its name from the fact that, unlike many other snakes, it has no markings on its underbelly. It eats mostly fish, crayfish, and salamanders and can be eaten by hawks and egrets. Have you ever seen a snake in the water?

Nerodia erythrogaster is a nonvenomous snake

Cooper's hawk

This bird of prey roosts in conifers (evergreen trees with cones), sleeping with its head tucked in. It will dash out between the trees to look for its next meal, often other birds; it kills its prey by capturing it with its feet and squeezing. Pretend your hands are talons and try to "catch" an imaginary bird with them.

Accipiter cooperii is a medium-sized hawk with a long tail—look for its silhouette in the sky

Texas skeleton plant

This perennial (blooms every year) flower with a pink or purple color blooms April through August. The name comes from its twiglike appearance. Some stems have no leaves and others have only a few small ones. If you find a Texas skeleton plant, draw the entire thing in your nature journal.

Lygodesmia texana

25

CRUISE TO CROCKETT GARDENS FALLS

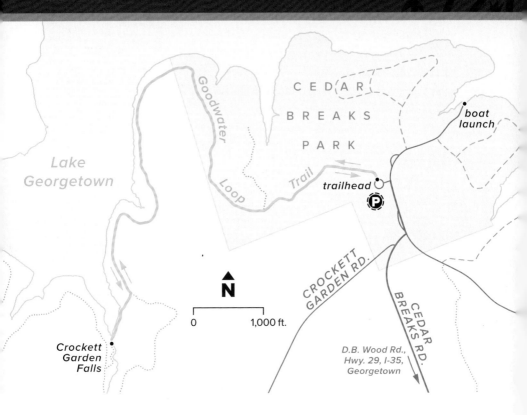

CEDAR

BREAKS

PARK

Goodwater

Loop

Trail

boat launch

trailhead

P

Lake Georgetown

CROCKETT GARDEN RD.

CEDAR BREAKS RD.

N

0   1,000 ft.

Crockett Garden Falls

D.B. Wood Rd., Hwy. 29, I-35, Georgetown

YOUR ADVENTURE

Adventurers, today you'll be hiking along the Goodwater Loop Trail, a 28-mile trail that loops around Lake Georgetown. These are the historical homelands of the Tonkawa people. Starting at the trailhead, you'll take a well-defined trail through a dense Ashe juniper forest. After about a third of a mile, you will hit a rocky downhill followed by a steep uphill. Climb the hill, continuing

Feel the cool spring water flowing at Crockett Gardens Falls →

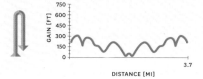

LENGTH 3.7 miles out and back

ELEVATION GAIN 321 ft.

HIKE + EXPLORE 3 hours

DIFFICULTY Moderate—Rocky
trail with a few tricky spots

SEASON Year round.

GET THERE Cedar Breaks Park is located on
Lake Georgetown. From Austin, take I-35 north
and Exit 261 toward Burnet. After exiting the
highway, turn left onto University Avenue.

After 1.2 miles, turn right onto D.B. Wood,
and after 2 miles left onto Cedar Breaks Rd.
Once you pass the entry station, take the first
left to enter the parking lot at the trailhead.

Google Maps: bit.ly/timbercrockett

RESTROOMS None at trailhead

FEE $5 day pass per vehicle (purchase online).
Be sure to reserve a day-use pass in advance.

TREAT YOURSELF Enjoy a refreshing
lemonade or full meal at Sweet Lemon
Kitchen, located on Georgetown Square,
5 miles southeast of the park.

Cedar Breaks Park
(877) 444-6777
https://www.swf-wc.usace.army.mil/
georgetown/Recreation/Parks/

straight to stay on the trail. After another quarter mile or so, Lake George-town will become visible in the distance. Once you get close to the lake, the trail takes a left turn so you are following the lake shoreline. A few minutes later, about one mile into the hike, you will spot limestone cliffs along the lakeshore. If you carefully climb down to the lake, this is a great place to stop for a swim or a power-up stop with a view. Once you are refreshed, continue on the trail. About a mile and a half into the hike, you'll see a bench on the left side of the trail. This is your cue to keep an eye out to make a right turn off the Goodwater Loop Trail and head down toward the lake. You will be able to see Crockett Gardens Falls in the distance. Once you reach the falls, take in the scenery and cool off in the spring-fed waterfall on a warm day. When you are ready to hit the trail again, pass the lake again and turn left to hop back onto Goodwater Loop Trail and head back the way you came.

SCAVENGER HUNT

Cedar sage

Cedar sage produces sweet flowers that are edible and beloved by hummingbirds and butterflies. On the other hand, deer tend to avoid this plant and other types of sage due to their smell. Can you smell the flowers? What do they smell like to you?

Salvia roemeriana loves to grow in the shade of Ashe juniper trees

Lake Georgetown

Lake Georgetown is a reservoir on the north fork of the San Gabriel River. You can hike around it using the Goodwater Loop Trail, which is 28 miles long. Campgrounds are along the way where one can spend the night if backpacking—an adventure that combines hiking with camping. If you were to go backpacking, what would you bring?

A view of Lake Georgetown from the hiking trail

Prairie verbena

Plants in the *Verbena* genus have been associated with the divine in some cultures. They were called "tears of Isis" in Ancient Egypt and "Hera's tears" in Ancient Greece. They believed the flowers sprang from divine tears and would bring about calmness and relaxation. What do you find calming or relaxing?

Glandularia bipinnatifida has a long flowering season, from March to October

Texas spiny lizard

These shy lizards have grey, black, white, or reddish-brown patterns on their backs to blend in with the trees they spend most of their time in. The male lizards have two blue streaks on their bellies. The males also have an unusual habit. When they are challenged by another male in a battle over territory, the two males have a push-up contest. Both of them do as many push-ups as they can until one of them gives up and runs away. Can you do ten push ups in a row? How many do you think a spiny lizard could do?

Sceloporus olivaceus is arboreal, meaning that it spends most of its time in trees

Crockett Gardens Falls

Early settlers to this area were drawn to the flowing natural spring. The land was acquired by James Knight in 1875, and the spring is named after him. He began a truck garden (vegetables to sell at a market) in 1879. Along with lots of vege-tables, he grew the first strawberries in William-son County. The farm was later purchased by R.M. Crockett, whom the falls are named after. Have you ever grown anything in your garden?

Crockett Gardens Falls is fed by a natural spring

26

HIKE THE SPRING LOOP AT BERRY SPRINGS PARK

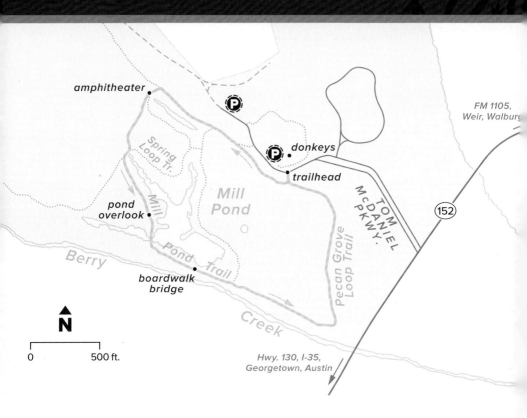

amphitheater

P

FM 1105,
Weir, Walburg

Spring
Loop Tr.

P • donkeys

• trailhead

pond
overlook •

Mill
Pond

TOM
MCDANIEL
PKWY.

152

Berry

Pond Trail

Pecan Grove
Loop Trail

boardwalk
bridge

Creek

N

0   500 ft.

Hwy. 130, I-35,
Georgetown, Austin

YOUR ADVENTURE

Adventurers, today you'll be hiking in a century-old heritage pecan grove.
This area is located on the historical homelands of the Tonkawa and Apache.
You'll start by heading right on the paved Pecan Grove Trail, turning left at
the amphitheater where the path turns to gravel. Veer right where the trail
splits passing Spring Loop Trail on your left. You'll soon see the spring-fed

A view of the Mill Pond at Berry Springs Park →

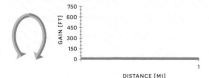

LENGTH 1-mile loop

ELEVATION GAIN 16 ft.

HIKE + EXPLORE 1 hour

DIFFICULTY Easy—Short and flat, with a stroller-friendly path

SEASON Year-round.

GET THERE From Austin, take I-35 north and use the Highway 130 Service Road free exit. After 0.8 miles, turn left onto County Road 152 for another 0.8 miles, then turn left onto Tom McDaniel Parkway to enter the park. After the park entrance, continue 0.3 miles to the parking lot and trailhead.

Google Maps: bit.ly/timberberrysprings

RESTROOMS At the parking lot near the trailhead

FEE Free

TREAT YOURSELF Enjoy an ice cream treat from a choice of 42 seasonally changing flavors at All Things Kids, an old-fashioned toy store with an ice cream and candy shop in the back. The store is located on the beautiful town square of Georgetown, 5 miles south of the park.

Berry Springs Park and Preserve
(512) 943-1920
Facebook @Berry-Springs-Park-And-Preserve/414035135279508
Instagram @FriendsofBerrySprings

Mill Pond. Hike toward the pond, then take a right for the path that runs alongside the water. Pass the Meadow Loop Trail, keeping the pond on your left. When you get to the aquatic viewing platform, take a moment to observe the pond, which is home to many species of fish and birds. Do you see any today? Next you'll cross a boardwalk. Continue to follow the hiking trail past the Mill Pond Loop on your left to stay straight on the Pecan Grove Trail. This will take you around the field of pecan trees back to the parking lot. At the end, you'll find an old farmstead and a barn with two donkeys. The donkeys enjoy visitors, so stop by to say hello! For an added adventure, spend the night at one of the campsites available at the park.

SCAVENGER HUNT

Osage orange

This deciduous (loses its leaves) tree produces a green fruit called an Osage orange or a horse apple. Although the fruit is not poisonous, it's also not edible. In fact, most foraging animals won't eat it. Only a few, such as squirrels and  deer, may nibble the tiny seeds inside the fruit. Millions of years ago, mastodons and mammoths are thought to have eaten these fruits, but they have long gone extinct. Some people think Osage oranges look a little bit like brains. What do you think? Sketch one in your nature journal.

Maclura pomifera ("pomifera" means "fruit-bearing" in Latin)

Pecan grove

Take a stroll through the pecan orchard and try to find some nuts on the ground. Pecans are edible and are often used in dessert recipes. Have you ever had pecan pie or pecan fudge?

Berry Springs is home to a century-old, historic pecan grove

Mealy sage

Mealy sage is native to the prairies and meadows of Texas and Mexico. It starts blooming in mid-April and continues until there's a winter freeze. The "mealy" part of the plant name comes from the word meal, meaning "a powdery substance made by grinding a grain into a powdery form" (for example, cornmeal). If you look closely at the mealy sage flower, there are powdery white felted hairs where the flower meets the stem, making them look "mealy."

Salvia farinacea is a perennial in the mint family

Historic compound

John had three children with his first wife, Betsy Smeathers. After she died, he married Gracie Treat and had three more children. After she died, he married Hannah Devore and the couple had twelve children together! John, Hannah, and their many young children moved to the land on Berry Creek in 1846, building and operating a spring-driven gristmill on the property.

The park is named for John Berry, a blacksmith, knifesmith, gunsmith, and furniture maker

Donkeys

At the end of the hike there's a small barn with two friendly donkeys named Lil' Bob and Pedro. You can go ahead and say hello, but please only feed them a handful of grass or hay. Feeding them more than that or anything else is not healthy for them. Have you ever fed a donkey before?

The donkeys at the park love visitors

ADVENTURES IN
PRAIRIES
AND LAKES

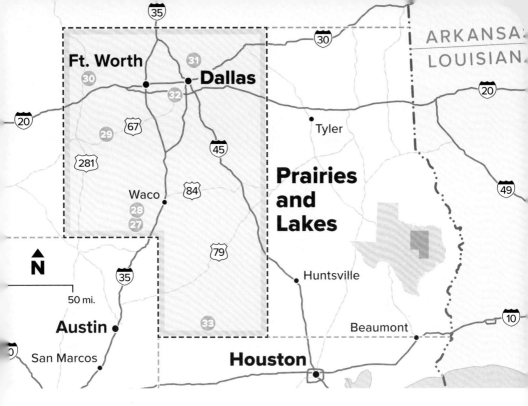

Adventurers,

placid landscapes of rolling hills, grasslands, and patches of woodland await you in the Prairies and Lakes region, which spans from north of Dallas/Fort Worth to south to the Waco area. This landscape marks the transition from the Panhandle Plains to the west and the Piney Woods to the east. Begin an hour north of Austin and continue north to Chalk Ridge Falls Park, where you'll explore a three-tiered waterfall and walk across an old suspension bridge. Your next three hikes will explore history as you check out a Tonkawa cave, dinosaur footprints at the Paluxy River, and a rocky canyon where, legend has it, cattle thieves once hid with their stolen goods. Your next two stops are close to Dallas. Check out a park featuring a beautiful waterfall and turtles galore, then go to a nature preserve featuring trails, a butterfly garden, a cattail pond, and plenty of wildlife. Your final adventure is just over two hours south of here—cap off your Prairies and Lakes adventures by spotting eagles at Lake Somerville. Let's go!

27

CHOOSE YOUR ADVENTURE AT CHALK RIDGE FALLS

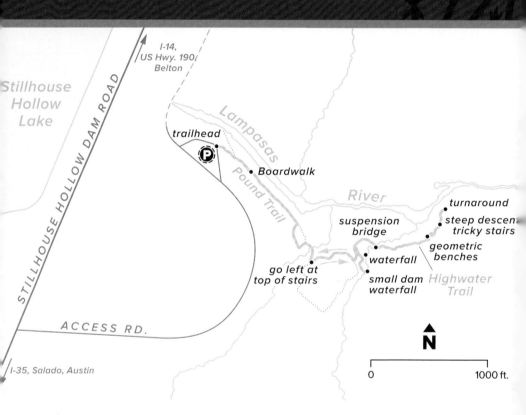

Stillhouse Hollow Lake

I-14, US Hwy. 190/ Belton

STILLHOUSE HOLLOW DAM ROAD

Lampasas

Pound Trail

trailhead

P

Boardwalk

River

suspension bridge

turnaround

steep descent

tricky stairs

geometric benches

waterfall

go left at top of stairs

small dam waterfall

Highwater Trail

ACCESS RD.

I-35, Salado, Austin

N

0   1000 ft.

YOUR ADVENTURE

Adventurers, today you'll swim under a waterfall and hike across an old suspension bridge as you explore part of the historical homelands of the Tawakoni. You'll start the hike on a gravel path and soon reach a boardwalk stretch. When you get to the top of a set of stairs, turn left to head directly toward the main attraction—the waterfall. (Turning right will also take

The park is named after these three-tiered falls →

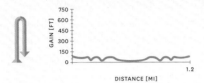

LENGTH 1.2 miles out and back

ELEVATION GAIN 90 ft.

HIKE + EXPLORE 1 hour

DIFFICULTY Moderate—A shorter adventure on a relatively flat trail that includes a couple of steep sections

SEASON Year-round. Summer is popular for swimming. Spring and fall offer cooler temperatures, fewer people, and more active wildlife. On warm days, bring a swimsuit to swim at the base of the falls.

GET THERE Exit I-35 and head west on FM 2484 for about a mile. Turn right onto FM 1670 and head north for 3.5 miles. Look for the park entrance on the right. Proceed 0.7 miles down the winding driveway to the parking area near the trailhead.

Google Maps: bit.ly/timberchalkridge

RESTROOMS At the parking lot

FEE Free

TREAT YOURSELF The Gin at Nolan Creek is a restaurant housed in an old cotton gin on the historic Bell County Courthouse Square. Grab some chips and queso dip.

Chalk Ridge Falls Park
(254) 939-2461
https://www.swf-wc.usace.army.mil/
stillhouse/Recreation/Parks/Corpsparks.asp

you to the waterfall, but indirectly.) Before you get to the waterfall the trail will take a sharp left turn on a hill. At the waterfall, it's time to swim and explore! You can also hike along the banks with the waterfall to your left. If you go upstream, you'll find a small dam with a shallow, less-crowded place to splash and play. When you're done, go back toward the waterfall and cross the suspension bridge. Stay on the path until a clearing with a set of geometric benches. This is a great turnaround point if you're ready to go. But if you want more water adventures, descend the steep, natural steps to the river. Then head back the way you came.

SCAVENGER HUNT

Suspension bridge

Suspension bridges like this one hold their weight with curved cables and vertical suspenders—can you spot those two parts of the bridge today? The earliest known version of suspension bridges was designed back in the fifteenth century by the architect Thang Tong Gyalpo. Amazingly, several of his bridges are still in use today! Would you call the one at this park stable or wobbly?

The suspension bridge provides a dry but wobbly passage over the water

Poison ivy

If you explore the woods, watch out for poison ivy. It is not actually poisonous, but you can get an itchy rash from it. This is the result of your skin touching the oily resin on the plant's leaves and stems. Make a sketch of a poison ivy plant in your nature journal, but don't touch it! Remember, "Leaves of three, let them be!"

It's a good idea to steer clear of *Toxicodendron radicans*

Chalk Ridge Falls

Approximately 140 million years ago, most of Texas was covered by seawater. As the sea level fell, limestone was exposed and became the canyon walls of Central Texas. The chalky rock left is referred to as "Austin Chalk." Today a spring-fed creek over these formations creates a beautiful waterfall that empties into Stillhouse Hollow Lake. After leaving the falls, how far away can you still hear the water?

These falls are fed by a spring

Great blue heron

When great blue herons are hunting, they wade slowly or stand in the water like statues. When they spot their meal, they wait for it to come into range and then throw their head forward quickly in a move called a "bill stab." They can also catch prey on land and in mid-air. You can spot a great blue heron in the air by the distinctive way it tucks its neck into its body in flight, creating an S shape. How long you can hold a heron pose?

Ardea herodias

Weir

The creek that feeds the waterfall is spring-fed. A short way upstream from the waterfall you'll find a weir (low dam). The notch in the cement is used to measure the flow of the creek. Visitors are welcome to play in the water but are not allowed to alter the flow of water through the notch. How is the water flow today?

If the plunge pool under the falls is too deep, try the shallower water in the creek above

28

POWER THROUGH THE CAVE, TOWER, AND POND LOOP

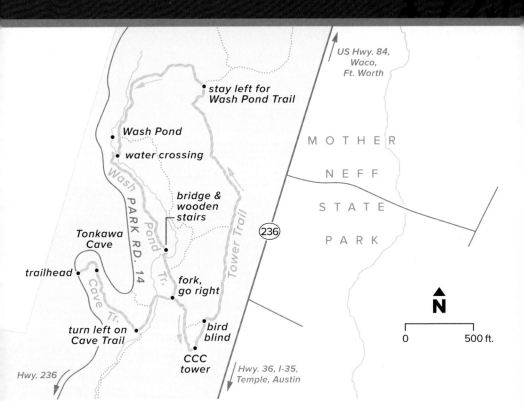

YOUR ADVENTURE

Adventurers, today you're trekking through one of the first state parks in Texas, where the dream of the Texas State Parks system was born. Isabella Eleanor Shepherd Neff's gift of six acres of land for a public gathering and recreation space gave rise to the movement in Texas, an effort led by her son, Governor Pat Neff. This area is the historical homeland of the Tonkawa.

Tonkawa Cave at Mother Neff State Park →

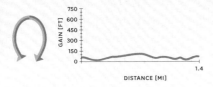

GAIN [FT]

750
600
450
300
150
0

1.4

DISTANCE [MI]

LENGTH 1.4-mile loop

ELEVATION GAIN 118 ft.

HIKE + EXPLORE 1.5 hours

DIFFICULTY Easy—Largely flat, with minimal rocky areas

SEASON Year-round. Spring is a beautiful time to see wildflowers.

GET THERE Mother Neff State Park is located about 30 miles southwest of Waco. The address is 1921 Park Road 14 in Moody. The entrance is on the northeast side of the park, entering from Highway 236. For this hike, drive 1.7 miles along the park road to the southern edge of the park where you'll find a small parking lot at the entrance to the Cave Trail.

Google Maps: bit.ly/timbermotherneff

RESTROOMS At the headquarters

FEE $2 for adults; free for children 12 and under; free with Texas State Parks annual pass. Be sure to reserve a day-use pass in advance, especially during peak seasons.

TREAT YOURSELF Grab a cupcake for the hike at Cuppiecakes, 11 miles up the road in McGregor.

Mother Neff State Park
(254) 853-2389
Facebook @MotherNeffStatePark
Instagram @MotherNeffSP

Your hike will begin on the Cave Trail, where a short stone stairway will lead you down to the Tonkawa Cave. On a hot day you'll see clusters of spiders cooling off on the cave walls. After that, you'll come to a fork in the trail. Go right on the Tower Trail to check out the Civilian Conservation Corps (CCC) tower, which is just a two-minute detour. When you get there, climb to the top for a nice breeze. Then return to the trail, where you'll soon reach the bird blind. For the next stretch you'll hike about 0.5 miles along a shady section, staying straight to avoid the Bluff Trail, which forks off to the left. Eventually you'll reach another fork—leave the Tower Trail here and go left onto the Wash Pond Trail. After 0.2 miles, you'll hop over a small water crossing before arriving at Wash Pond. If you're ready for a breather, there's a bench overlooking the water that's perfect for a snack break. When you're ready, hike another 0.5 miles back toward the cave, turn right on the Tower Trail, and return to where you started. At the top of the stone steps, take a moment to celebrate another completed hike!

SCAVENGER HUNT

Wash Pond

Legend holds that the pond got its name when settlers began washing their laundry in it. In the 1930s, workers from the Civilian Conservation Corps (CCC) built a dam that turned the pond into a swimming hole. Today the water serves as a lifeline for plant and animal communities, and swimming is no longer permitted—unless you're a fish or a frog! The spring that feeds the pond  often dries up in the summer months, but can run through the entire canyon in the park during times of plentiful rainfall. Pretend you are a woodland animal. Can you think of a few places you could get water to drink?

This small natural pool sustains life for local plants and animals

Tonkawa Cave

For thousands of years this land was inhabited by Indigenous people. Rock overhangs like this one provided shelter from the elements. It was also close to a source of water, the Leon River. What else would you add to this cave to make it suitable to live in?

During summer months, you can find insects and other critters enjoying the cooler temperatures in the cave

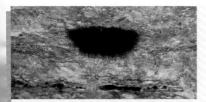

Harvestmen

These arachnids are also known as daddy long-legs and look like spiders, but they aren't. They have no silk glands, so they cannot spin webs. They also lack segmented bodies, fangs, and the ability to produce venom. Check for huge clusters of them, called congregations, under the rocky ledges of Tonkawa Cave. Have you ever huddled together with your family while on an outdoor adventure? Write about it or draw a picture in your nature journal.

Opiliones

CCC tower

This impressive tower was built using materials from the park property. Limestone rocks created strong foundations and beautiful walls. The tower was built as an observation deck. Try climbing up to the top to feel the breeze on a warm day and enjoy the forested views year-round. Can you count the number of steps going up?

It took the Civilian Conservation Corps four years (1934 to 1938) to build this observation tower

29

FIND THE DINO TRACKS AT DINOSAUR VALLEY

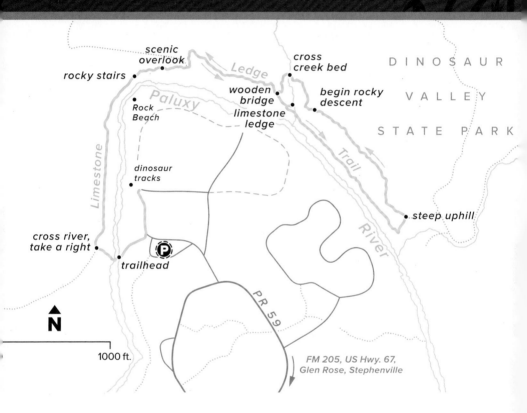

scenic overlook

rocky stairs

Ledge

cross creek bed

DINOSAUR

wooden bridge

begin rocky descent

VALLEY

Paluxy

Rock Beach

limestone ledge

STATE PARK

Limestone

dinosaur tracks

Trail

cross river, take a right

River

steep uphill

trailhead

PR 59

N

1000 ft.

FM 205, US Hwy. 67, Glen Rose, Stephenville

YOUR ADVENTURE

Adventurers, today you'll travel back in time 100 million years to when dinosaurs roamed the shallow seas of Central Texas. You'll have a chance to check out real dinosaur tracks left by theropod and sauropod dinosaurs! This is the historical homeland of the Wichita, Comanche, and Tonkawa. Park at the Main Dinosaur Track Site and take the paved walkway to the

The Paluxy River is home to real dinosaur tracks →

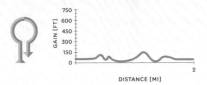

LENGTH 2-mile lollipop

ELEVATION GAIN 160 ft.

HIKE + EXPLORE 1.5 hours

DIFFICULTY Moderate—Some steep and rocky sections but otherwise flat

SEASON Year-round. If you hike in summer, start early to beat the heat. You do need to cross the river, so you may want to bring water shoes.

GET THERE The park is located 4 miles west of Glen Rose. Take Route 67 to FM 205 for 4 miles to Park Road 59, then head a mile to the headquarters. Follow the signs to Main Dinosaur Track Site and park there.

Google Maps: bit.ly/timberdinovalley

RESTROOMS At the headquarters and near the playground

FEE $7 for adults; free for children 12 and under; free with Texas State Parks annual pass. Be sure to reserve a day-use pass in advance, especially during peak seasons.

TREAT YOURSELF Grab a popsicle or ice cream treat from the park store, located near the dinosaur models.

Dinosaur Valley State Park
(254) 897-4588
Facebook @DinosaurValleyPark
Instagram @DinoValleySP

river on the Paluxy River Trail. Hop across a few rocks to get to the dinosaur footprints. Once you've explored the dinosaur tracks, you'll need to get to the other side of the river to start your hike. To do this, head back up the paved path until you reach a fork in the trail. Turn right for the beginning of the Limestone Ledge Trail. It begins with a shallow river crossing. On either side of the crossing, the water gets deeper, so this is a great place to stop for a swim. On the other side of the river, you'll hit the trail. Walk along flat grassland for the first 0.5 miles of the hike, then begin your ascent with some rocky steps. The scenic overlook with a bench is a beautiful spot to stop for a snack break. Stay right on this section of the trail, bypassing the Overlook Trail and continuing on the Limestone Ledge Trail. A small wooden bridge marks the beginning of the loop portion of your lollipop hike—stay straight once you cross the bridge. This trail is called the Limestone Ledge Trail for a reason. Check out the cool formations to your left. Climb up to take a look! Continue for another 0.5 miles before making a couple of sharp left turns for the return. This is where it gets rocky and a bit steep. Toward the end you'll cross a riverbed (dry in summer) and arrive back at the wooden bridge. Repeat the first part of the trail—and take another dip! Don't forget to check out the big dinosaur models by the headquarters before you leave.

SCAVENGER HUNT

Theropod tracks

The theropod tracks at the park are thought to come from a dinosaur relative of *Tyrannosaurus rex*. It was a large biped (stood on two feet) dinosaur, about 20 feet tall and 25 feet long. Measure out 25 feet and imagine a dinosaur this huge traipsing around here!

Three-toed *Acrocanthosaurus* tracks; An artist's rendering of what these dinosaurs looked like

Sauropod tracks

Sauropods were over 70 feet long and 13 feet high at the shoulder, with a long neck stretching up from there. An adult human would have been too short even to reach the dinosaur's knees! They left tracks that look a lot like elephant footprints, but larger. The hind feet prints are over a yard long; those of the front feet were smaller, clawless, and horseshoe-shaped. Find a spot to make a footprint of your own. Does yours have anything in common with the dinosaurs'?

Sauroposeidon proteles walked on four legs

Paluxy River Scenic Overlook

From here you can see the Paluxy River on its 38-mile journey to the Bravos River. When the dinosaurs were alive, it was covered by a shallow sea. The tracks were first discovered by a local teenager named George Adams who was wandering around the river area. What do you think remains to be discovered in nature where you live?

Bird's-eye view of the Paluxy River

Limestone ledge

Limestone has been around for millions of years and has been used by humans for thousands of years. The pyramids at Giza in Egypt and the Colosseum in Rome, Italy, are made of limestone. What would you build out of limestone?

This trail is named after limestone ledges like the one you see here

30

PEEK INTO HISTORY AT PENITENTIARY HOLLOW

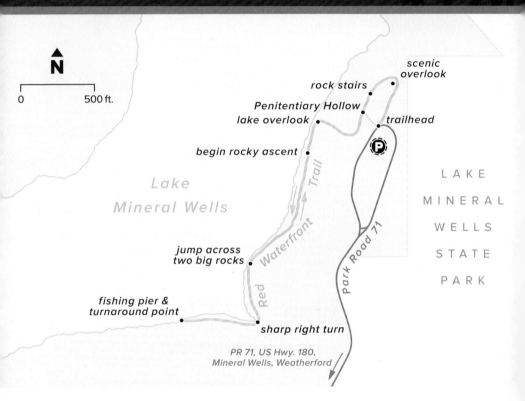

YOUR ADVENTURE

Adventurers, today you'll explore a rocky canyon where cattle thieves once hid with their stolen goods. On the beautiful historical homelands of the Comanche, you'll begin your hike at the archway sign marking Penitentiary Hollow. Follow the trail to the scenic overlook and take a moment to enjoy views of the lake. When you're ready, head down the rock stairs to the huge

Lake Mineral Wells offers a swimming area for cooling off after a summer hike →

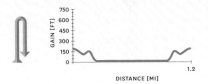

LENGTH 1.2 miles out and back

ELEVATION GAIN 187 ft.

HIKE + EXPLORE 1 hour

DIFFICULTY Moderate—A few ups and downs to navigate

SEASON Year-round.

GET THERE The park is located 4 miles east of Mineral Wells on Highway 180. Take the park road for 2.1 miles past the park entrance, following the signs for Penitentiary Hollow and the Red Waterfront Trail (located in the southeast corner of the park). The road will dead-end at the trailhead parking lot.

Google Maps: bit.ly/timbermineralwells

RESTROOMS At the parking lot

FEE $7 for adults; free for children 12 and under; free with Texas State Parks annual pass. Be sure to reserve a day-use pass in advance, especially during peak seasons.

TREAT YOURSELF The Trailway Trading Post near the lake has popsicles, ice cream, and other delicious treats to enjoy after your hike.

Lake Mineral Wells State Park & Trailway
(940) 328-1171
Facebook @LakeMineralWells

sandstone rock formations that make up a small canyon. This spot is filled with cool rocks, so take your time exploring. When you're ready to move on, you'll continue on the Red Waterfront Trail, beginning a rocky ascent. You'll jump across a couple of rocks, take a sharp right turn, and soon see a wooden fishing pier. This is your turnaround spot and a great place to have a snack by the lake before hiking back. On a warm day, make sure you check out the swimming area at the park before heading home! Consider staying at one of the park campgrounds to make a weekend of it.

SCAVENGER HUNT

Lake Mineral Wells Overlook

Lake Mineral Wells is named after the mineral water that is said to have cured locals in the late 1800s of ailments like rheumatism (joint diseases). Mineral Wells became a world-renowned health resort and tourist attraction that used the slogan, "Where America Drinks Its Way to Health." Today it is a wonderful place to swim, but like most lakes, the water is not meant for drinking. Be sure to fill up your water bottle at a drinking fountain instead!

Check out the view of Lake Mineral Wells

Penitentiary Hollow

Two huge sandstone rock formations create a unique geological feature resembling a small canyon. The source of the name "Penitentiary Hollow" is not certain, but legend has it that the area is named after cattle thieves who hid here with their stolen goods and were often caught and sent to the penitentiary. Today the area is a popular spot for rock climbers. Another interesting highlight is the four towering elms growing in the canyon. Can you find all four?

Look for the four towering elms growing out of the rocky floor

Blanchard's cricket frog

These amphibians (live on land and water) prefer to live along the edges of shallow, permanent bodies of water like lakes and ponds. The tiny frogs are both nocturnal (active during the night) and diurnal (active during the day), especially in warmer months. In the coldest months they hibernate. Do your sleeping patterns differ in summer compared to winter?

Acris blanchardi is a small frog, only about an inch long

Channel catfish

Look closely at its whiskers that give it its name—there are eight. They are called barbels and are sensors for locating food like plankton and insect larvae. Can you draw something in your nature journal that looks like a dogfish? Or a mousefish?

Ictalurus (means "fish cat" in Greek) *punctatus* (means "spotted" in Latin) is one of the predominant fish species here

Canyon wren

These songbirds make their homes in the rocky canyons of western North America. Here in the Lone Star State, their range is mostly limited to West Texas, but they also live in Penitentiary Hollow. They hunt for insects in the crevices of the rocks, using their long, slender beaks to grab

their prey. These songbirds cling to rock walls and can even scale vertical surfaces with ease. If you could choose a superpower of either flying or being able to climb around on vertical surfaces, which would you choose?

Catherpes mexicanus is a small, pot-bellied, rust-colored bird with a white throat and chest

31

HIKE THE HUCK FINN TRAIL

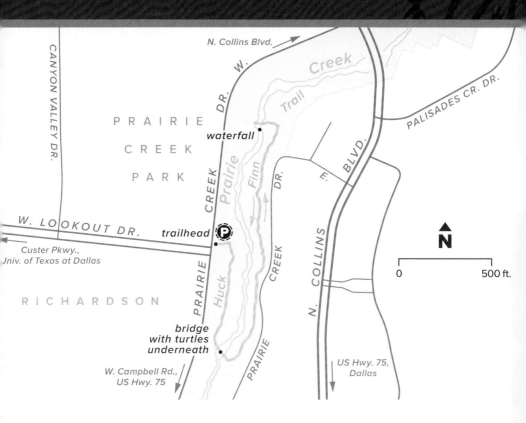

YOUR ADVENTURE

Adventurers, today you'll be exploring the historical homelands of the Caddo, Wichita, and Comanche in an urban park that was once a family farm. The land was owned by the Campbell family, one of Richardson's most prominent founding families. Shortly before World War II, the Campbell family grew concerned about food shortages that might arise during

The waterfall on the Huck Finn Trail →

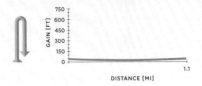

LENGTH 1.1 miles out and back

ELEVATION GAIN 55 ft.

HIKE + EXPLORE 1 hour

DIFFICULTY Easy—Flat, stroller-friendly path

SEASON Year-round.

GET THERE Prairie Creek Park is located in Richardson, 18 miles north of Dallas. From Dallas, take Route 75 north, then turn left on West Campbell Road. Turn right (going north) when you reach West Prairie Creek Drive. The hike begins at a small parking lot on the corner of West Prairie Creek Drive and West Lookout Drive.

Google Maps: bit.ly/timberhuckfinn

RESTROOMS None

FEE Free

TREAT YOURSELF Grab a hamburger, veggie burger, or milkshake at Hat Creek Burger Company, 0.5 miles east of the park (this is also a good place to use the restroom). The restaurant offers an outdoor seating area with a playground.

Prairie Creek Park
(972) 744-4300

the war. In just 24 hours, the family constructed a concrete dam and bridge that would allow passage over Prairie Creek and provide water for cattle and crops. The original dam was converted into a waterfall in the late 1990s when it became clear that it would need significant repairs. You'll start your hike at the intersection of West Lookout Drive and West Prairie Creek Drive. Begin by turning right on the Huck Finn Trail to hike toward the bridge that crosses Prairie Creek. Stop in the middle of the bridge to take a peek into the water below. Can you spot any turtles or other wildlife? After you cross the bridge, turn left. Around the 0.5-mile mark of your hike, the waterfall will be on your left. Take a few minutes to continue to walk down to the river, until you reach the end of the trail.

SCAVENGER HUNT

Red-eared sliders and other turtles

Prairie Creek is home to many turtles, including plenty of red-eared sliders. These reptiles get their name from the small, distinctive, red stripe around their ears. Their hard upper shell, or carapace, has lots of nerves running through it, so these turtles are sensitive to touch. If you scratch a turtle shell, it will feel like it does for a human when someone scratches their skin. Red-eared sliders can walk at a speed of about 3 miles per hour on land—that's pretty fast for a turtle, don't you think? How long would it take one to do the hike you're doing today?

Trachemys (means "rough turtle" in Latin) *scripta elegans*

Wood duck

Texas is home to two groups of wood ducks. Young birds that were born here during spring and summer generally remain in Texas year-round. Other wood ducks migrate from colder climates and stay in Texas only for winter. Would you prefer to live in a different place in summer and winter or in one place all year?

Aix sponsa males have green, crested heads, a spotted chest, and black and white stripes; the females have gray heads

Waterfall

Today the waterfall is a picturesque spot to take photos or experience a moment of peace in nature, but in the 1940s it was an important source of water for a family farm. The waterfall was originally a dam that was built to help the family's food supply as World War II approached. Close your eyes and listen to the sounds of rushing water for one whole minute. Do you feel calmer after opening your eyes again?

The waterfall is near the north end of Prairie Creek Park

Black walnut

The native species of trees at the park have been marked with QR codes so that you can learn more about them as you hike. Black walnut is one of the most valuable hardwoods. Walnut trees produce round, hard-shelled nuts that feed animals as well as humans and drop to the ground in fall. If you find one on the ground, take a closer look. It may have a hard hull or casing; inside will be the actual nut, which contains the tree's seed. Do you like to snack on nuts? What is your favorite kind?

Juglans nigra

32

TOUR THE CATTAIL POND

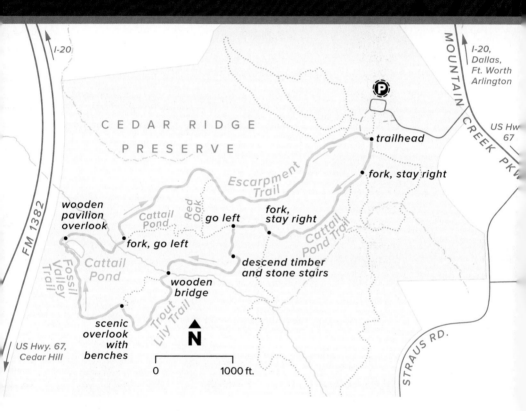

YOUR ADVENTURE

Adventurers, today you'll be hiking where the Blackland Prairie meets a limestone escarpment (a long, steep slope). This place has it all—scenic views, shaded forest paths, beautiful wildflowers, and birdwatching opportunities galore. This is the historical homeland of the Wichita, Comanche, Caddo, and Cherokee. Nowadays the Audubon Society works to preserve

The overlook at Cattail Pond →

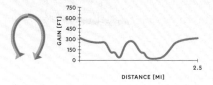

GAIN [FT]

DISTANCE [MI]

LENGTH 2.5-mile loop

ELEVATION GAIN 321 ft.

HIKE + EXPLORE 2 hours

DIFFICULTY Challenging—Rocky stretches and a few spots with steep elevation gain

SEASON Year-round. Closed Mondays. Beautiful yellow and orange foliage in fall; colorful spring and summer wildflowers.

GET THERE From downtown Dallas, take I-35E to Route 67, then turn right onto Danieldale Road. After 3 miles you'll pass Clark Road, at which point Danieldale Road becomes Mountain Creek Parkway. From here, continue a mile before turning left to enter Cedar Ridge Preserve. In 0.3 miles you'll reach the parking lot and trailhead.

Google Maps: bit.ly/timbercedarridge

RESTROOMS At the entrance

FEE Free; $5 donation encouraged

TREAT YOURSELF Enjoy a frozen yogurt treat at YummiBerry, 3 miles southeast on FM 1382.

Cedar Ridge Preserve
(972) 709-7784
Facebook @CRPAudubonDallas

the land for wildlife. Start out on the Cattail Pond Trail. You'll pass two forks for the Possumhaw Trail and one for the Cedar Brake Trail before descending a set of timber-and-stone stairs—power up at the benches you pass. You'll pass another fork of the Cedar Brake Trail then cross a wooden bridge, staying straight to continue on the Cattail Pond Trail. Turn left at the Fossil Valley Trail and get ready to do some climbing! You'll soon reach another set of timber-and-stone stairs. Power up at the next bench you come to before crossing a wooden bridge, staying left as you come upon a scenic overlook. After that, you'll begin your descent as you hike toward Cattail Pond. Take a break at the wooden pavilion overlooking the pond, and power up for the final mile of the hike. Shortly after the pond, the trail will fork again. Turn left after the wooden bridge to take the Escarpment Trail. You'll stay straight on this trail the whole way back, passing the Red Oak Trail on your right. There will be one more steep climb, then a short flat stretch back to the trailhead.

SCAVENGER HUNT

Butterfly garden
A sign at the butterfly garden lists eleven different species of butterflies (and moths) you may find at the preserve, including the giant swallowtail. This insect has big black wings with yellow dots and bands—the bottom of its wings are forked, which is why they're named after a bird, a swallow. How many different kinds of butterflies can you spot in the garden today?

Check out the butterfly garden near the trailhead; Giant swallowtail, *Papilio cresphontes*

Cattail Pond

The Cattail Pond is a great place to look for turtles, birds, and other wildlife, and a perfect spot to stop for a snack. While you're powering up with some food and water, try to be as quiet as possible to bring out more wildlife. What creatures do you think live around here?

The pond may look still, but it's full of life

Violet ruellia

You can find these wildflowers blooming in summer. The purple trumpet-shaped flowers last for a single day, opening at dawn and closing again by afternoon. Each flower has the same number of petals—can you count how many?

Ruellia nudiflora

Water moccasin

One way to identify this rare, semiaquatic reptile is to look at the placement of its body when it's swimming. Water moccasins swim with their whole body afloat so they can observe their environment. Most nonvenomous snakes, on the other hand, swim with only their head above the

water. Water moccasins can also dive underwater when looking for prey. Outside of the water, you may find them lounging on rocks or logs near the water's edge—do not approach them, though, because their bite is both painful and venomous. Fully grown ones can reach up to 5 feet long. If you lie down, how long are you compared to an adult water moccasin?

Agkistrodon piscivorus is a venomous water snake that lives near shallow marshes and ponds

33

KEEP AN EYE OUT FOR EAGLES AT LAKE SOMERVILLE

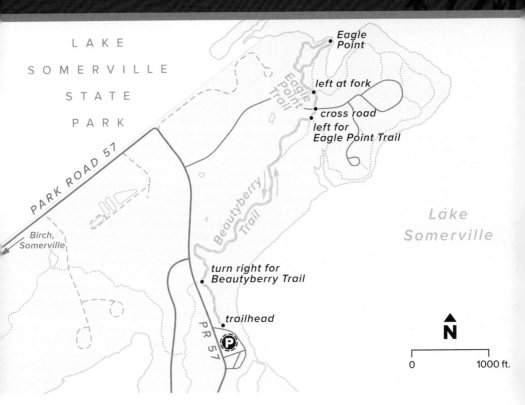

LAKE

SOMERVILLE

STATE

PARK

PARK ROAD 57

Birch,
Somerville

Eagle
Point

left at fork

cross road

left for
Eagle Point Trail

Eagle Point Trail

Beautyberry Trail

Lake
Somerville

turn right for
Beautyberry Trail

trailhead

PR 57

N

0   1000 ft.

YOUR ADVENTURE

Adventurers, welcome to the historical lands of many native people,
including the Tonkawa and Tawakoni. This area is home to plenty of wildlife, including the bald eagles that nest here. The park is divided into two
sections—you'll be exploring the Birch Creek Unit today. Start at the trailhead for the Beautyberry Trail and follow the trail for about a mile. As you

Bald eagles make their home at Lake Somerville →

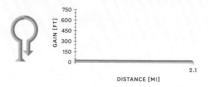

DISTANCE [MI]

LENGTH 2.1-mile lollipop

ELEVATION GAIN 18 ft.

HIKE + EXPLORE 1 hour

DIFFICULTY Easy—A flat
path through the park

SEASON Year-round. In spring the
trail is covered with flowers.

GET THERE From Highway 290, take
Highway 36 north. Turn left onto Highway 60
and travel approximately 8 miles before

turning left on Park Road 57. You'll reach the
park in 4 miles. Park at the trailhead, located
at the Somerville Lake Boat Ramp.

Google Maps: bit.ly/timbersomervillepark

RESTROOMS At the parking lot

FEE $5 for adults; free for children 12 and
under; free with Texas State Parks annual pass

TREAT YOURSELF Grab an ice cream
treat at the Lake Somerville State
Park Birch Unit Headquarters.

Lake Somerville State Park and Trailway, Birch
Creek Unit
(979) 535-7763
Facebook @BirchCreekStatePark
Instagram @LakeSomervilleSP

approach the mile marker, you'll cross a small road to continue toward the Eagle Point Trail. Soon you'll run into a fork. Go left for the Eagle Point Trail, which is a short lollipop section ending at the lake. Once you reach the end, there is a picnic table under a large oak tree. This is a perfect place to take a snack break and scan the sky for eagles before you make your way back to the trailhead. For an overnight adventure, book a Lake Somerville campsite and wake up to soaring eagles!

SCAVENGER HUNT

Lake Somerville

This body of water was constructed by the US Army Corps of Engineers in June 1962 to control the frequent flooding here. It covers 11,630 acres and has an 85-mile shoreline. The new lake ended the flooding that had destroyed many homes, farms, and businesses in Somerville, although it also put some other lands under water. It also created a popular spot for recreational activities. What's your favorite thing to do at a lake?

Many creeks drain into this reservoir, including Nails Creek, Yegua Creek, and Birch Creek (where you are today)

Bald eagle

Sightings of this majestic bird of prey are common here. Male and female eagles collaborate to build nests in trees. Sometimes they continue adding to the same nest for years, eventually creating a giant one. Bald eagles are not actually bald. They are born with brown feathers covering their heads and bodies, and as they mature the brown feathers are replaced with white ones. Does your hair change color as you grow?

Haliaeetus leucocephalus (means "white" and "head" in Latin)

Maroon blanketflower

The rare maroon blanketflower grows in sunny conditions in sandy soils. The origins of the name "blanketflower" is a small mystery. Some believe it comes from the resemblance the flowers bear to brightly colored and patterned blankets made by some Native Americans. Others say it comes from its ability to cover the ground with a blanket of color. Can you think of another possible explanation?

Gaillardia amblyodon has been found only in Texas

Differential grasshopper

A differential grasshopper is only about 2 inches long, but it can jump about 30 inches. That means it is able to jump 15 times the length of its own body! If you could do that, how much distance would you cover in a jump?

Melanoplus differentialis is considered a pest in most places

Little bluestem grass

Little bluestem is named after the bluish color of the stem during spring. By fall, the stems have typically reached about 3 feet tall and turn a vibrant reddish-tan color, with white seed tufts sticking up at the top. The seeds are a source of food for birds in winter. Measure yourself against the grass today—are you taller than it?

Schizachyrium scoparium

ADVENTURES IN
THE PINEY
WOODS

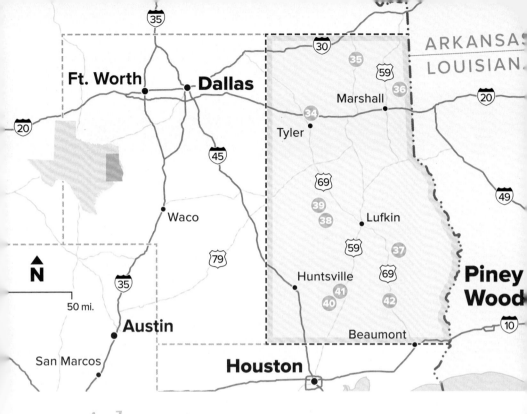

Adventurers,

welcome to the majestic Piney Woods, a forest ecosystem that spans the eastern parts of Texas as well as Louisiana, Arkansas, and Oklahoma. Begin in the northeast, just 90 minutes from Dallas. You'll start by forest bathing among the 100-foot-tall trees at Tyler State Park and then continue northwest to Daingerfield State Park to enjoy spring wildflowers or fall foliage. Next, head to the banks of the Big Cypress Bayou on the Louisiana border. At Caddo Lake State Park, hike or rent a kayak or canoe and view the towering trees of the world's largest cypress forest. Two hours south in the Angelina National Forest, visit the ruins of a historic sawmill and hike part of the 20-mile-long 4-C trail. See the first mission in Texas, built by the Spanish in 1690 and now part of Mission Tejas State Park. In the Sam Houston National Forest, sample the Lone Star Hiking Trail, the state's longest continuous footpath. At Lake Livingston State Park, walk on a beautiful mile-long boardwalk. Then head to Big Thicket National Preserve, home to four of the five types of carnivorous plants found in North America. Let's get started!

34

TREK AMONG THE TALL TREES OF TEXAS

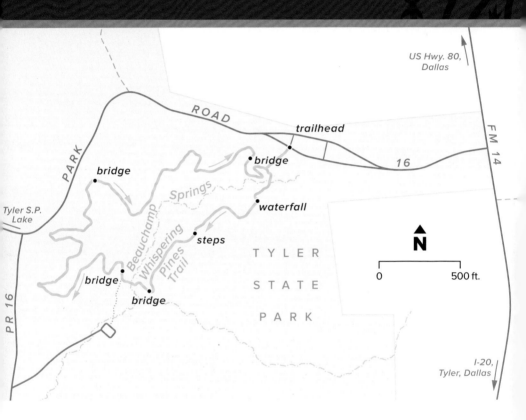

YOUR ADVENTURE

Adventurers, today you'll be walking amongst 100-foot-tall pines on the historical homelands of the Caddo. This park offers a rare opportunity to see what the East Texas woods looked like before the landscape was dramatically altered by logging and farming. You'll start your hike at the Whispering Pines trailhead. A few steps into the hike, the trail splits. Take

Do some forest bathing among majestic 100-foot-tall pines →

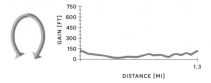

GAIN [FT]

750
600
450
300
150
0

1.3

DISTANCE [MI]

LENGTH 1.3-mile loop

ELEVATION GAIN 121 ft.

HIKE + EXPLORE 1 hour

DIFFICULTY Easy—Shorter, fairly flat

SEASON Year-round. Spring boasts blooming wildflowers and fall has stunning foliage colors. During both spring and fall, you may see migrating animals such as birds, bats, and butterflies visiting the park.

GET THERE Tyler State Park is located 2 miles north of I-20, north of Tyler. After entering the park by turning onto Park Road 16, you'll pass the headquarters. The trailhead is just 0.1 miles ahead, on the left.

Google Maps: bit.ly/timbertylertalltrees

RESTROOMS At the headquarters near the trailhead

FEE $6 for adults; free for children 12 and under; free with Texas State Parks annual pass. Be sure to reserve a day-use pass in advance, especially during peak seasons.

TREAT YOURSELF Enjoy some tacos or guacamole at C Rojo's Taqueria in Tyler, 3 miles down the road from the park.

Tyler State Park
(903) 597-5338
Facebook @TylerStatePark

the left fork to go clockwise around the loop and see the CCC-constructed waterfall below Beauchamp Spring, a natural spring at the top of the hill. Tree growth has resulted in a low water table; on hot summer days, large trees require a whopping 1000 gallons of water! The hiking path is clearly defined so you won't get lost in the woods. A few small bridges along the way take you across creeks and marshy areas. Follow the trail for a mile, observing the trees and wildlife, and you'll make it back to the trailhead. When you're done, be sure to check out the 64-acre spring-fed lake or snag a campsite for an overnight adventure.

SCAVENGER HUNT

Shortleaf pine

Shortleaf pines are big trees with long, straight trunks and short needles. These big trees have surprisingly small cones; they measure only 1½ to 2½ inches high, with scales sticking out. Can you find a tree that is too big to wrap your arms around?

Pinus echinata grows up to 120 feet tall, but its cones are the smallest of any pine in Texas

Rock waterfall

The CCC built this park between 1935 and 1941, constructing roads, planting trees, and even making this waterfall. The clay-and-rock dam held the water produced by the springs to form a beautiful lily pond, located in the middle of the family picnic grounds. Excess water from the pond spills over the top of the dam and down the rocks, creating a waterfall that is pleasing to both eyes and ears. If you had a chance to build a big park for people to enjoy nature, what would you include?

This rock waterfall was built by the Civilian Conservation Corps (CCC)

Flowering dogwood

In fall these deciduous (loses its leaves) trees produce bright red berries that are poisonous to humans but provide food for birds and other animals. In spring they produce large, white flowers with four petal-like leaves called bracts that protect many tiny, greenish or yellow flowers inside. Look closely to see if you can see beyond the bracts into the actual flowers.

Cornus florida blooms in early spring

Raccoon

The English word "raccoon" comes from the indigenous Virginia Algonquin word *aroughcun*, which means "animal that scratches with its hands." It's not a good idea to get too close to a wild animal, but when you get home look up a picture of raccoon paws. Do they look like your hands?

Procyon lotor

Brown-headed nuthatch

This small bird feeds high in the shortleaf pine canopy and has a call that sounds like a squeaky toy. They are a social species and members of the same family can be found sitting next to each other on branches, grooming each other's feathers. They also raise families cooperatively.

In addition to the parents, there are usually one to three helper birds that contribute to building and defending the nest and feeding the young. How do you help each other in your family?

Sitta pusilla

35

REVEL IN THE RUSTLING LEAVES

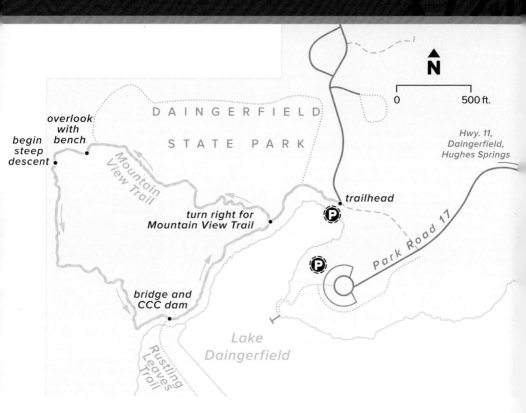

YOUR ADVENTURE

Adventurers, today you'll be exploring 507 acres of the Piney Woods of Texas, on the historical homelands of the Caddo. The CCC used the natural springs to build an 80-acre lake that serves as the focal point of the park. It was largely made with hand tools! When you're touring the park, you'll still see many of the structures the CCC constructed, including a scenic road,

A scenic view of Daingerfield State Park Lake →

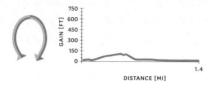

GAIN [FT]

750
600
450
300
150
0

1.4

DISTANCE [MI]

LENGTH 1.4-mile loop

ELEVATION GAIN 118 ft.

HIKE + EXPLORE 1.5 hours

DIFFICULTY Easy—Mostly flat with some roots across the path

SEASON Year-round. Spring offers blooming wildflowers and fall offers colorful foliage.

GET THERE From Dallas/Fort Worth, take I-30 E to Mt. Pleasant and take Exit 160; follow State Highway 49 to Daingerfield State Park (about 22 miles from I-30). Check in at the headquarters then continue along the park road, turning right at the original CCC entrance sign into the park. The trailhead parking is on the left after a bend in the road.

Google Maps: bit.ly/timberdaingerfield

RESTROOMS At the headquarters and further up the road, across from the Cedar Ridge Camping Area

FEE $4 for adults; free for children 12 and under; free with Texas State Parks annual pass. Be sure to reserve a day-use pass in advance, especially during peak seasons.

TREAT YOURSELF Enjoy a sandwich or Sunday brunch after the hike at Mug Shots, 3 miles northwest of the park along Highway 11. (Closed on Saturdays.)

Daingerfield State Park
(903) 645-2921
Facebook @DaingerfieldStatePark
Instagram @DaingerfieldSPTexas

Bass Lodge, retaining walls, culverts, steps from the combination building, parking curbs, and of course, trails. Your hike starts on the Rustling Leaves Trail, which quickly reaches a fork with the Mountain View Trail. Turn right and follow the trail until you reach a scenic overlook with a bench. Stop here for a quick power-up break. You'll then begin a steep descent. The trail heads straight as it levels out, then meanders till you reach a wooden bridge and the CCC dam. Stop here to observe turtles, birds, and maybe even a fish or two jumping out of the water. You'll reach another fork with the Rustling Leaves Trail. For an extra adventure, you can take a right here. The trail winds around a small peninsula where you'll see a grill remaining from the CCC era. This detour adds about another 1.5 miles to your journey. As you continue along the trail, keep an eye out for the birds that live here, including red-tailed hawks and bald eagles. When the trail lets out at the beach area, walk up a slight hill toward the combination building. From there you'll see the trail-head as you finish your hike across the meadow. For still more adventure, rent a paddleboat, canoe, or kayak and spend the night at a Daingerfield State Park campsite. Saturdays offer seasonal programming for kids!

SCAVENGER HUNT

Red fox

These small mammals are sometimes confused with gray foxes, even though they are distant cousins in the dog family Canidae. The two types of foxes do share several characteristics—they live in similar habitats and both can have patches of gray and red fur. To tell them apart, look at the color at the tip of the tail. Gray fox tails have black tips and red fox tails have white tips. What is a characteristic that makes you stand out from your cousins?

Vulpes vulpes is a member of the dog family

Eastern red cedar

Did you know that some species of trees have separate male and female trees? Eastern red cedars are an example of this. When they bloom in late winter, female trees produce green flowers and male trees produce yellow ones. In fall, you can find little quarter-inch cones produced by male trees and small blue-gray ones on female trees. Find a berry on the ground and smash it up. What does it look like inside??

Juniperus virginiana is resistant to drought, heat, and cold

CCC grill

The men of the CCC thought the peninsula was a good spot for a picnic, so they constructed grills and tables here. The view across the lake provides a view of the historic combination building that the CCC also constructed. Today only one grill remains, at the end of the penin-sula. Can you find it?

The CCC used local timber, stone, and concrete here

Longleaf pine

Longleaf pines and loblolly pines are both com-mon in the Piney Woods region of East Texas. One way you can tell the difference between them is by looking at the needles. Longleaf pines have extra-long needles, about 12 inches in length, and these stay green all winter. Loblolly pines have needles that are about half as long and usually turn brown in winter. Can you find both types of trees and needles on your hike?

Pinus palustris reaches heights of 100 feet or more

36

BRIDGE HOP THE CADDO FOREST TRAIL

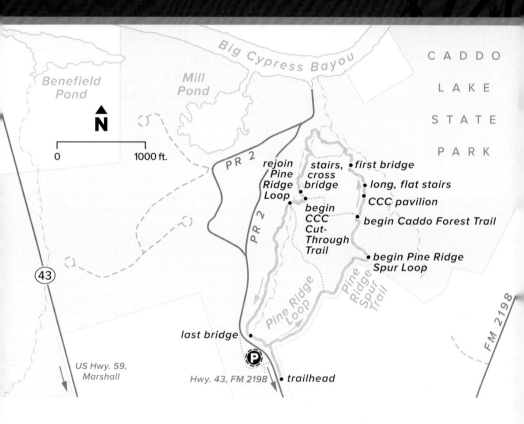

Big Cypress Bayou

CADDO

LAKE

STATE

PARK

Benefield
Pond

Mill
Pond

N

0   1000 ft.

PR 2

PR 2

rejoin
Pine
Ridge
Loop

stairs,
cross
bridge

• first bridge

• long, flat stairs

• CCC pavilion

begin
CCC
Cut-
Through
Trail

• begin Caddo Forest Trail

• begin Pine Ridge
  Spur Loop

Pine Ridge Spur Trail

Pine Ridge
Loop

FM 2198

43

last bridge •

ℙ

US Hwy. 59,
Marshall

Hwy. 43, FM 2198   • trailhead

YOUR ADVENTURE

Adventurers, today you'll visit a fairy-tale forest full of tall trees and wooden
bridges on the historical homelands of the Caddo. Start at the Pine Ridge
Loop trailhead. After 0.25 miles, the trail will split. Take the right path,
following the sign for the Pine Ridge Loop. Stay straight onto Pine Ridge
Spur Loop. Around the 0.5-mile mark the trail will split again. Go right on the

The Piney Woods ecoregion of East Texas offers beautiful fall hiking →

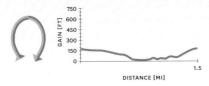

GAIN [FT]

750
600
450
300
150
0

1.5

DISTANCE [MI]

The trailhead is located 0.3 miles from the park entrance on the right.

Google Maps: bit.ly/timbercaddo

RESTROOMS At the headquarters

FEE $4 for adults; free for children 12 and under; free with Texas State Parks annual pass. Be sure to reserve a day-use pass in advance, especially during peak seasons.

LENGTH 1.5-mile loop

ELEVATION GAIN 183 ft.

HIKE + EXPLORE 1 hour

DIFFICULTY Easy—A shorter, mostly flat trail

SEASON Year-round.

GET THERE Travel north of Karnack for a mile on Highway 43 to FM 2198, then go east for 0.5 miles to Park Road 2.

TREAT YOURSELF Grab a fried alligator appetizer or burger at Big Pines Lodge, 2 miles up the road (FM 2198) from the park.

Caddo Lake State Park
(903) 679-3351
Facebook @CaddoLakeSP

Caddo Forest Trail and follow the sign for the boat ramp to head toward the CCC pavilion. After checking out the pavilion, go down the stairs and cross a small wooden bridge to continue your hike. Cross several more bridges on the Caddo Forest Trail, eventually reaching a small road. Before the road, turn left, staying on the Caddo Forest Trail. At the next bridge, the trail forks— stay right to continue on the trail. Cross two more bridges and reach a set of steps leading up to a cross-timber bridge. After crossing, turn right for a brief jaunt on the CCC Cut-Through Trail. Cross one more cross-timber bridge then turn left to connect with the Pine Ridge Loop again. The last stretch of the hike is uphill and single-file, so help the little ones. You'll cross one final wooden bridge. After, check out Caddo Lake for an adventure with a secluded, mystical feel. It's home to the largest bald cypress tree forest in the world. It's also home to alligators, so watch out!

SCAVENGER HUNT

Shortleaf pine

The bark of the shortleaf pine starts out very dark when the tree is young and turns reddish brown over time. The bark appears scaly because it grows in large, thin plates. Compare the bark of a shortleaf pine to that of a black walnut tree. What differences do you notice?

Check out the bark of *Pinus echinata*

Black walnut

The bark of this deciduous (loses its leaves) tree is usually a grayish color, but if you can find a spot where some of the bark has come off, there's a rich chocolate-brown color under-neath. The bark consists of rough ridges that run up and down the tree (vertically). Take a piece of paper in your nature journal, use a crayon or pencil, and make a bark rubbing.

Check out the bark of *Juglans nigra*

American alligator

Be alert for alligators if you visit this lake after your hike. Alligators were classified as an endangered species under the passage of the Texas Endangered Species Act of 1973 but have made an amazing comeback. A fun fact about alligators is that their front feet have five toes, while their rear feet have only four webbed toes. Can you guess which toes are better at helping an alligator move swiftly through the water?

This park is home to *Alligator mississippiensis*, the largest reptile in the state

CCC pavilion

During the hot summer months of 1933, CCC workers built the first structures and trails on this land. The pavilion was one of many structures built here. The others included nine large cabins and a recreation hall. The buildings were built to harmonize with the natural beauty of the local area. The interiors were finished with pine, oak, and hickory harvested from the upland forests of the park land, and native iron ore was used for the fireplaces and foundations, all built by CCC workers.

The Civilian Conservation Corps (CCC) built this pavilion in the 1930s

Prothonotary warbler

These yellow birds with blue-gray wings are usually found along waterways foraging for insects. You may hear them before you see them due to their loud, ringing song. Pretend you're a warbler and forage for insects on the tree—do you see any?

Protonotaria citrea is a small songbird that migrates to Caddo Lake each spring

37

SURVEY THE HISTORIC SAWMILL RUINS

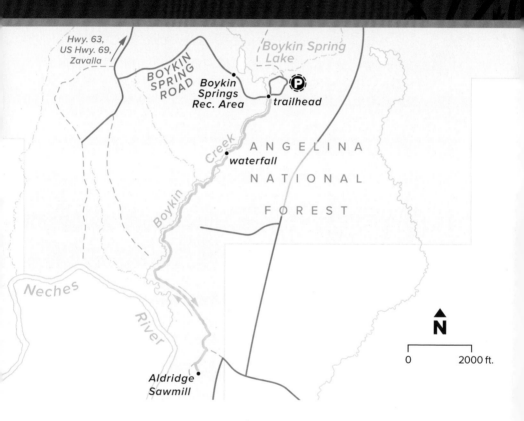

Hwy. 63,
US Hwy. 69,
Zavalla

BOYKIN SPRING ROAD

Boykin Spring Lake

Boykin Springs Rec. Area

(P) trailhead

Creek

waterfall

A N G E L I N A

N A T I O N A L

F O R E S T

Boykin

Neches

River

Aldridge Sawmill

N

0   2000 ft.

YOUR ADVENTURE

Adventurers, today you'll be going back in time to an era when the Angelina National Forest was a bustling lumber powerhouse, producing more than 75,000 feet of lumber boards every day. Before that era, this was the historical homelands of the Caddo. Begin at the trailhead for the Sawmill Hiking Trail. It's 2.5 miles to Old Aldridge, the ruins of the old sawmill: 5 miles out and

The ruins of the Old Aldridge Sawmill in the Angelina National Forest →

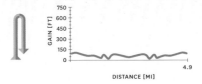

LENGTH 4.9 miles out and back

ELEVATION GAIN 121 ft.

HIKE + EXPLORE 2.5 hours

DIFFICULTY Challenging—A longer route, but the terrain is flat and manageable

SEASON Year-round.

GET THERE From Zavalla, follow Highway 63 for 11 miles. Turn right (south) on Forest Road 313 for 2.5 miles to Boykin Springs Recreation Area, then follow signs for the Sawmill Hiking Trail. You'll pass the fee station (there's no need to stop unless you're camping overnight), pass a parking lot on your right, then turn left. Continue until you reach a parking area with a picnic shelter and restroom. The trees are marked with yellow blazes for the 0.1-mile walk to the trailhead.

Google Maps: bit.ly/timbersawmill

RESTROOMS At the parking lot

FEE Free

TREAT YOURSELF Grab a donut or some kolaches from DeeDee's Donuts, 14 miles up the road on Highway 36.

Boykin Springs Recreation Area
(936) 897-1068

back. So make sure you're equipped with good hiking shoes, water, and snacks. About 0.5 miles into the hike, there's a small waterfall on the right; it's easy to miss, so take some time to listen as you reach this part of the hike. About a mile from the trailhead you'll cross a small road. Follow the sign pointing toward Old Aldridge. At about 2.25 miles into the hike, you will see a red spray-painted sign for the sawmill. Stay right to get there, then explore the ruins and imagine what this spot would have been like 100 years ago. Can you see how nature is reclaiming the old buildings? What do you think it will look like in another 100 years? When you're ready, hike back to the trailhead. For an additional adventure, book a campsite at nearby Caney Creek or Sandy Creek.

SCAVENGER HUNT

Waterfall on Boykin Creek

Boykin Creek is named after Sterling Boykin, who moved to Texas with his children in the 1840s. In an area with millions of acres of tall trees, he somehow found this beautiful spot with an unending supply of cool, clear water. Local Indigenous people may have helped him find it. Put a leaf in the water and imagine it floating onward to the 416-mile-long Neches River, which empties into the Gulf of Mexico.

A small, refreshing waterfall on the trail

Orange jelly fungus

This jiggly orange fungus makes a colorful appearance on logs any time of year during wet weather. It looks like jelly laying there, but it's attached to the wood by a white stalk. If you find one, give it a tug to get a peek at the anchoring stalk.

Dacrymyces capitatus

Eastern North American destroying angel

The common name "destroying angel" doesn't sound very friendly, and there is a good reason for that. This gilled mushroom is highly toxic. On the other hand, it's perfectly safe to look at it. Tell a grown-up if you spot one in the woods. Stand back and try to sketch it in your nature journal.

Amanita bisporigera is a very poisonous mushroom!

Pinewood gingertail mushroom

This species of gilled mushroom is not poisonous (but is too bitter to eat), so it's safe to check them out. When an individual is young, its cap is bell-shaped, with raised middle and outer edges that curve downward, making it resemble a little bell. As it gets older, the outer edges expand and rise and the center falls inward, which some people think resembles a belly button. What do you think?

Xeromphalina campanella

Aldridge Sawmill Historic Site

Between 1905 and 1923 the sawmill was a large and bustling operation. This era is referred to as the "bonanza" period of East Texas logging. It was brought about by massive population growth and industrialization in the northern parts of the country, which depleted the lumber in those areas and thus created demand for southern lumber. Unfortunately, sawmill operations were often crowded and unsafe. The mill burned to the ground for the first time in 1911. It was rebuilt, but after several more fires and the depletion of local forests, the mill shut down for good.

The sawmill was first constructed by Hal Aldridge in 1905

38

FROLIC THROUGH THE DAVY CROCKETT NATIONAL FOREST

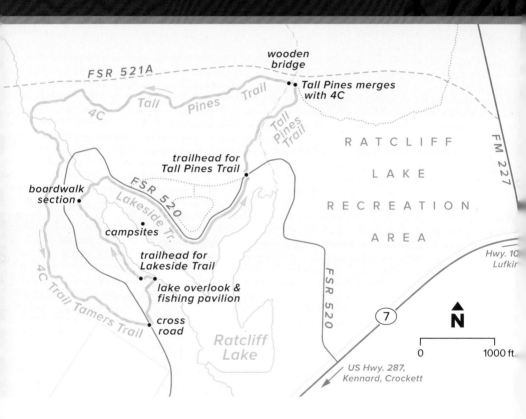

FSR 521A

Tall Pines Trail

4C

wooden bridge

Tall Pines merges with 4C

Tall Pines Trail

RATCLIFF

LAKE

RECREATION

AREA

FM 227

trailhead for Tall Pines Trail

boardwalk section

FSR 520

Lakeside Tr.

campsites

trailhead for Lakeside Trail

4C Trail Tamers Trail

lake overlook & fishing pavilion

cross road

Ratcliff Lake

FSR 520

Hwy. 10 Lufkir

7

N

0   1000 ft.

US Hwy. 287, Kennard, Crockett

YOUR ADVENTURE

Adventurers, put on your explorer hats because today you'll be hiking through the Davy Crockett National Forest, named after an American frontiersman. These lands are the historical homelands of the Caddo. You'll begin with the blue-blazed Tall Pines Trail—the trailhead is on the north side of the road. You'll merge with the 4C Trail, marked with white

A view of Ratcliff Lake →

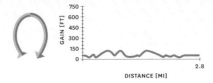

LENGTH 2.8-mile loop

ELEVATION GAIN 137 ft.

HIKE + EXPLORE 1.5 hours

DIFFICULTY Easy—Flat, good for all skill levels

SEASON Year-round.

GET THERE From Lufkin, take Highway 103 west for 16 miles to where it merges with Highway 7. Continue west for 12 miles and turn right at the entrance to the recreation area. Then continue 1.5 miles on Forest Service Road 520 until you reach the trailhead for the Tall Pines Trail. There is a small parking lot at the trailhead.

Google Maps: bit.ly/timberdavycrockett

RESTROOMS At the nearby Loblolly Loop, and you'll also pass some mid-hike

FEE $5 per vehicle; cash or check using self-pay envelope

TREAT YOURSELF Grab some fried catfish or peach cobbler or at The Country Church Cafe, located 3.6 miles down the road from the recreation area, in Kennard.

Ratcliff Lake Recreation Area
(936) 655-2299

blazes, about 0.25 miles into the hike. Cross the wooden bridge then follow the hiking path marked by the joint blue and white blazes until you reach the other trailhead for the Tall Pines/4C Trail. At this point you'll need to cross the road and walk past the restrooms to get to the dock overlooking Ratcliff Lake. After taking a few minutes to enjoy the view, continue left for the signed Lakeside Trail. You'll eventually turn right to connect briefly with the Trail Tamers Trail and walk along a beautiful boardwalk before completing the final stretch of the hike near a set of campsites. The sites will get sparser as you approach the walk-in campsites toward the end of the hike. Once you're done, consider heading back to camp there for the night.

SCAVENGER HUNT

Yaupon holly
This evergreen (doesn't lose its leaves) shrub produces bright red berries in fall that are an important food source for many species of birds and mammals. It's one of only two known native plants in the United States that produces caffeine. Some people prefer to drink yaupon tea instead of coffee. Do your family members prefer to drink coffee or tea?

Ilex vomitoria gets its name from the incorrect belief by European settlers that ingesting the berries caused vomiting

Tree stump chair
Tree stump carving can result in lots of creative artwork, including sculptures of animals and other figures, patterns, or even furniture. This tree stump looks like a chair. If you had a tree stump, what would you carve it into? Each ring shows a year of that tree's life. Look closely—can you guess why some rings would be skinny and others wider?

Try sitting on this tree stump chair

Fox squirrel

Look for these mammals with excellent vision and well-developed senses of hearing and smell. They use a variety of sounds and noises to communicate with each other, including barks, chatters, screams, and whines. They can also communicate by scent marking. If you wanted to try to communicate with a squirrel, what method of communication would you try? Communicate nonverbally with your hiking buddy now.

Sciurus niger is a member of the rodent family

False turkey tail fungus

This fungus looks a lot like a turkey tail fungus, but it's actually an entirely different species. You can tell the difference between false turkey tail and the real thing by checking the underside. True turkey tail is white underneath the cap and has lots of small holes in it, called pores. False

turkey tail has more of a tan color underneath and its surface is completely smooth. Check underneath the cap to figure out which kind you've found.

Stereum ostrea grows horizontally out of rotting wood

Ratcliff Lake

This 45-acre lake was once a source of water for the Central Coal and Coke Company sawmill, which operated here from 1902 to 1920. Sawmills used water for steam power, firefighting, and a place to store logs without drying them out. They also transported logs on the water. Have you ever taken a log ride at a water park?

Ratcliff Lake was built in 1936 by the Civilian Conservation Corps (CCC)

39

FIND THE MYSTERIOUS CCC BATHTUBS

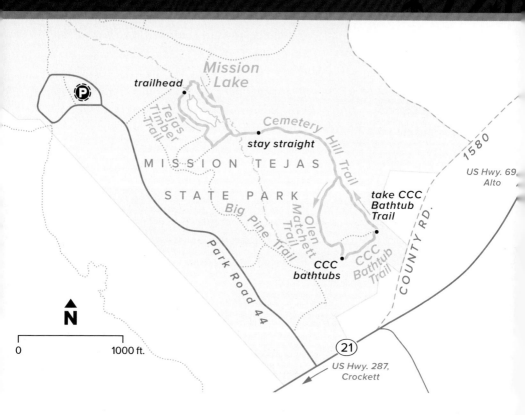

trailhead

Mission Lake

Tejas Timber Trail

Cemetery Hill Trail

stay straight

MISSION TEJAS

STATE PARK

Big Pine Trail

Olen Matchett Trail

take CCC Bathtub Trail

1580

US Hwy. 69, Alto

COUNTY RD.

CCC Bathtub Trail

CCC bathtubs

Park Road 44

N

0   1000 ft.

21

US Hwy. 287, Crockett

YOUR ADVENTURE

Adventurers, get ready to dive deep into Texas history as you hike among the tall trees at this 1930s-era Civilian Conservation Corps camp that's on the historical homelands of the Caddo. Welcome to Mission Tejas State Park, the home of the first mission in Texas, built by the Spanish in the late-1600s as part of an effort to counter French settlements. You'll begin

Follow this trail to an unsolved mystery →

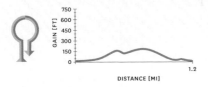

GAIN [FT]

750
600
450
300
150
0

1.2

DISTANCE [MI]

LENGTH 1.2-mile double lollipop

ELEVATION GAIN 200 ft.

HIKE + EXPLORE 1 hour

DIFFICULTY Easy—Relatively flat, fine for all skill levels

SEASON Year-round.

GET THERE The park is located 21 miles northeast of Crockett and 12 miles west of Alto on Highway 21. The entrance to the park is in Weches, where Park Road 44 intersects Highway 21. From the park entrance, continue along the park road, turning right after about 0.5 miles to reach the playground. Park near the playground and walk over to the Tejas Timber trailhead.

Google Maps: bit.ly/timbermissiontejas

RESTROOMS At the nearby playground

FEE $3 for adults; free for children 12 and under; free with Texas State Parks annual pass

TREAT YOURSELF Enjoy some donuts at Donut Palace, 13 miles northeast of the parking area along Highway 21.

Mission Tejas State Park
(936) 687-2394
Facebook @MissionTejasStatePark
Instagram @MissionTejas

your hike at the trailhead for the Tejas Timber Trail. Just a few steps into the hike you'll encounter a fork. Stay left, following the sign for the CCC bathtubs. Soon the trail will fork again—stay right here as you pass by the Chimney Loop Access Trail. Remain on the Tejas Timber Trail, continuing straight as you pass a fork on the right. Follow the sign pointing you toward the CCC bathtubs and turn left to merge with the Cemetery Hill Trail. You'll stay straight at the Lightning Trail and the Olen Matchett Trail, both of which will be on your right. A half-mile into the hike, stay on the lookout for the much-advertised bathtubs. When you find them, step into one and imagine taking a bath here. Would it be comfortable? Where would the water come from? When you're done with the bathtubs, continue on the Olen Matchett Trail, then turn left when you reach the sign for Cemetery Hill Trail to make your way back to the trailhead. When you reach the Tejas Timber Trail, turn left for a trip around the other side of Mission Lake (also called the CCC Pond) to complete your hike. When you're done, check out the playground and consider making a weekend of it by camping at the park.

SCAVENGER HUNT

Eastern coral snake

This venomous reptile can be recognized by its bands of red, yellow, and black that repeats in a pattern. Remembering the pattern helps to distinguish venomous coral snakes from harmless, nonvenomous scarlet king snakes that have black bands in between the yellow and red ones. There is a rhyme to help you remember this: "Red touch yellow, kill a fellow / Red touch black, venom lack." Can you remember the rhyme? Be careful and look down as you walk to ensure you don't accidentally step on one.

Brightly colored *Micrurus fulvius* is dangerous

CCC Pond/Mission Lake

You can fish for catfish, bass, and sunfish in this pond. For hundreds of years, the Caddo lived here, fishing in the river and harvesting corn, beans, melons, and squash. Can you imagine finding all your food in nature instead of at a grocery store?

The CCC built a pond near the playground and picnic area

Black willow

Look for these deciduous (loses its leaves) trees with a long history of medical use. Ancient people made tea from willow bark and used it to treat stiff joints and ease other aches and pains. By the middle of the 1800s, scientists called chemists had discovered that the pain-relieving effects came from a chemical in the bark called salicin, which is similar to aspirin. If you were going to be a scientist when you grow up, what kind of scientist would you want to be?

Salix nigra thrives in wet areas

CCC bathtubs

The origin of these structures remains a mystery to this day. Their name comes from their bathtub-like appearance, but no one knows what they are. It's unlikely they were used for bathing because the CCC had fully equipped barracks about a mile away. What do you think these structures could have been used for?

These features are called "the CCC bathtubs," but no one knows what their real purpose was

40

HIT THE LONE STAR HIKING TRAIL

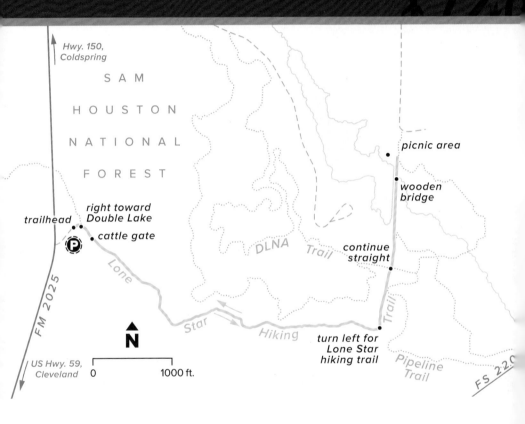

YOUR ADVENTURE

Adventurers, today you'll be hiking on the longest continuous footpath in Texas—the 129-mile Lone Star Hiking Trail, which winds through the Sam Houston National Forest on the historical homelands of the Atakapa. You'll begin your hike at Lone Star Trailhead #11 and turn right to head toward Double Lake Recreation Area. You'll pass through a small cattle guard, and

Are you ready to tackle a couple miles of this 129-mile trail? →

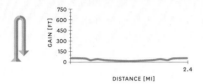

LENGTH 2.4 miles out and back

ELEVATION GAIN 56 ft.

HIKE + EXPLORE 1.5 hours

DIFFICULTY Easy—A level hike
suitable for all ages and skill levels

SEASON Year-round.

GET THERE From Highway 59 in Cleveland,
take FM 2025 north 17 miles and turn
right at Double Lake. About a mile south
of the entrance sign for the Double Lake

Recreation Area there is a small parking
lot for Lone Star Hiking Trail's Trailhead
#11. You'll start your hike here.

Google Maps: bit.ly/timberlonestar

RESTROOMS Near the hike's turnaround
point at Double Lake Recreation Area

FEE The Lone Star Hiking Trail is free;
$7 per vehicle for day-use pass at
Double Lake Recreation Area

TREAT YOURSELF Enjoy a burger or wrap
and try strawberry cheesecake in a mason
jar for dessert at The Mason Jar Bar & Grill,
4 miles north of the park in Coldspring.

Double Lake Recreation Area
(936) 344-6205
Facebook @DoubleLake

about 0.75 miles into the hike you'll turn left, following the sign for the Lone Star Hiking Trail. Continue straight on this trail until you reach the lake. Cross the bridge to reach the picnic area—enjoy lunch here with a view of Double Lake before beginning your hike back. The park also offers swimming, fishing, mountain biking, and camping, so there are plenty of opportunities for more adventures.

SCAVENGER HUNT

Red-cockaded woodpecker

The red-cockaded woodpecker makes its home in longleaf, shortleaf, and loblolly pine trees. It pecks a hole in the trunk to create a cavity, scaling loose bark out of its way. These holes are sometimes reused by other animals such as owls, squirrels, and even honeybees. Not including humans, how many different kinds of animals (not just pets) do you think live in your house?

Leuconotopicus borealis eats insects it finds in the bark of trees

Winter russula mushroom

The winter russula mushroom is named *russula* for its red color and *emetica* for the stomach aches it causes when eaten raw. However, the toxicity can be eliminated by pickling or par-boiling (partially boiling). It was widely popular in Eastern European countries and Russia, but most experts today do not recommend eating it. Have you ever eaten a pickled vegetable or other pickled food? Was it sweet or sour?

Russula emetica is also known as "The Sickener"

Double Lake

You can fish, swim, boat, and picnic right on this 23-acre lake. There are three fishing piers, plus a boat ramp for boats with small electric motors. There are also canoe rentals available seasonally. Have you ever been canoeing?

Double Lake is stocked with bass, bream, and catfish

Longleaf pine

These evergreens (don't lose their leaves) once covered nearly 100 million acres but now cover only a tiny remnant of that area. Early European settlers cleared entire forests of longleaf pines to make room for settlements and to sell lumber used to build railroad and ships. It seemed like there was a never-ending supply, but by the 1920s, many were gone and replaced with faster-growing pines like loblolly or slash pines. Can you find different types of pine trees in this park?

Sad to say, *Pinus palustris* now covers only 3% of its original range

Green tree frog

As their name suggests, these frogs are tree dwellers, but they also need clean water, so they are often found near ponds, lakes, and other wetlands. Most can jump more than 5 feet. They can change color. They are a vivid lime green while they are warm and active, but may turn olive green, brown, or gray when cool and resting. Can you guess why this would be helpful to them?

Dryophytes cinereus

41

HOP ON BOARD THE PINEYWOODS BOARDWALK

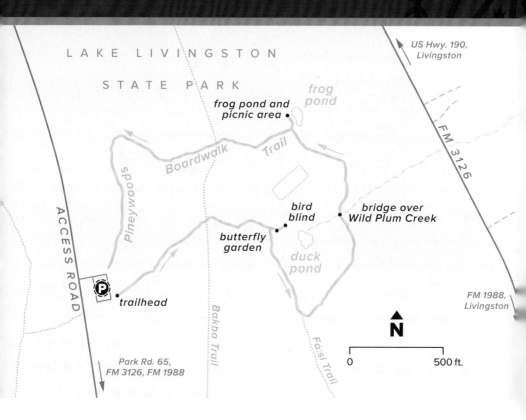

YOUR ADVENTURE

Adventurers, today's hike takes you over wetlands and through the woods as you trek through the historical homelands of the Orcoquisacs, Bidai, and Deadose. This hike stands out because you'll be on a boardwalk the whole time. Begin your hike with the trail on the right. Stay straight at the first junction, crossing Bakba Trail. You'll soon run into the duck pond, monarch

Today's whole hike is on a boardwalk →

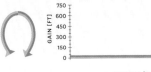

GAIN [FT]
750
600
450
300
150
0
                    1
DISTANCE [MI]

LENGTH 1-mile loop

ELEVATION GAIN 13 ft.

HIKE + EXPLORE 1 hour

DIFFICULTY Easy—A short boardwalk hike

SEASON Year-round. Some of the best wildlife viewing is in winter, when the foliage is not as thick.

GET THERE The park is a mile south of Livingston on Highway 59. Travel 4 miles west on FM 1988 and 0.5 miles north on FM 3126 to Park Road 65. Check in at the headquarters. Turn right after the headquarters, then turn right to continue 0.5 miles to the first parking lot on your right, where you'll find the Pineywoods Boardwalk trailhead.

Google Maps: bit.ly/timberlakelivingston

RESTROOMS At the headquarters and at each camping area

FEE $6 for adults; free for children 12 and under; free with Texas State Parks annual pass. Be sure to reserve a day-use pass in advance, especially during peak seasons.

TREAT YOURSELF Enjoy a cappuccino with a grilled PB&J or "cake balls" at The Bull Shack Coffee & Smoothies, located 5 miles northeast of the park in Livingston.

Lake Livingston State Park
(936) 365-2201
Facebook @LakeLivingstonSP

butterfly waystation, and wildlife-viewing area. At the wildlife-viewing area, you'll find a poster showing the many different sizes and shapes of beaks that various birds use to find and eat different types of food. If you were a bird, what kind of beak would you want? When you're done observing, continue along the boardwalk. Soon after crossing a bridge over Plum Creek, you'll reach the frog pond. Most frogs are active after dark, so if you take an evening hike you'll hear an amphibian symphony. Stay straight when you reach the Bakba Trail again and you'll soon arrive back where you began. Consider spending the night camping at Lake Livingston State Park for an overnight adventure.

SCAVENGER HUNT

Pileated woodpecker

This bird reaches up to 20 inches in length, with a 30-inch wingspan—that's big for a woodpecker! It gets its name from the Latin word *pileated*, meaning "capped," because the woodpecker looks like it's wearing a red cap. Try to listen for the thump-thump-thump of it pounding its hard, sharp beak into bark looking for yummy insects to eat. Then try to look for signs of these birds—trees with holes all over the trunk.

Dryocopus pileatus is the largest woodpecker species in Texas

Turk's cap

You can find Turk's cap flowers blooming in Texas from May through November—a long period. This plant is Texas-tough! It can grow in full sun or full shade and in wet or dry soil. The red flowers produce a nectar that is delicious to hummingbirds, butterflies, and even humans. Have you ever tasted flower nectar?

Malvaviscus arboreus is a member of the hibiscus family

Coyote

These canines are usually most active at dawn and dusk but can also be nocturnal, meaning they are active at night. Even if you cannot see a coyote, you may be able to hear one. Coyotes have complex communication patterns and howl for several reasons. One is to bring pack members

back together after they have been out hunting individually. Another is to mark a pack's territory from other coyotes who may be in the area. What do you think you could communicate to another human by howling?

Canis latrans is a member of the dog family

American mink

These mammals make their homes in hollow logs or by digging in the ground, so keep your eyes open for signs of their homes. Sometimes they add grass or leaves to make it cozier. Have you ever built a hideout outside?

Neovison vison lives along riverbanks and lakeshores

Loblolly pine

The loblolly pine (also called bull pine or rosemary pine) is the largest of the southern pines. It has a long, straight trunk, dark green needles, and narrow, reddish-brown cones that often appear in pairs. Loblolly pine cones are spiky and open in hot, dry weather and close in cold, moist

weather. If you find an open pine cone, try bringing it home and soaking it in water, simulating moist weather. Test whether it closes as a result! The word "loblolly" means "mud puddle," and the tree is named for the low, wet places it often grows in, although it can be found in drier places as well.

Pinus taeda

42

CATCH A GLIMPSE OF CARNIVOROUS PLANTS

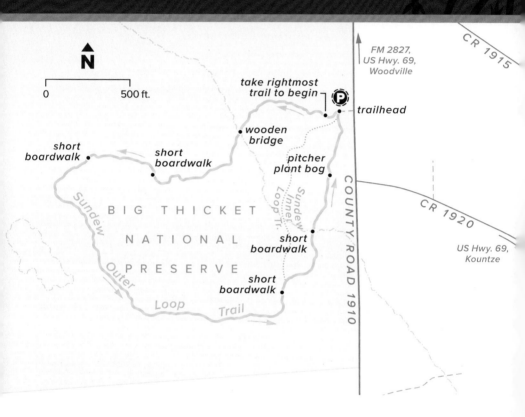

N

0   500 ft.

take rightmost
trail to begin

trailhead

FM 2827,
US Hwy. 69,
Woodville

CR 1915

wooden
bridge

short
boardwalk

short
boardwalk

pitcher
plant bog

BIG THICKET

NATIONAL

PRESERVE

Sundew Inner Loop Tr.

Sundew

Outer

Loop   Trail

short
boardwalk

short
boardwalk

COUNTY ROAD 1910

CR 1920

US Hwy. 69,
Kountze

YOUR ADVENTURE

Adventurers, today you'll traipse through the Big Thicket, one of the most
ecologically diverse parts of North America and the historical homeland of
the Alabama-Coushatta. Here eastern hardwood forests meet coastal plains
and midwestern prairies—that means a lot of plant and animal life for a
small area. One of the plants you'll see is the trail's namesake, the sundew

Stroll the wooden boardwalk through a forest of pines and ferns →

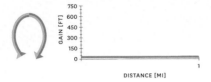

GAIN [FT]

750
600
450
300
150
0

DISTANCE [MI]

1

LENGTH 1-mile loop

ELEVATION GAIN 22 ft.

HIKE + EXPLORE 30 minutes

DIFFICULTY Easy—A short, level walk in the woods

SEASON Year-round.

GET THERE The trailhead is about 4 miles south of Warren and 14 miles north of Kountze. From Route 69/287, head west on FM 2827, then turn left (south) onto County Road 1910. Continue 0.2 miles to the Sundew Trail parking area, where you'll park close to the trailhead.

Google Maps: bit.ly/timbersundew

RESTROOMS At the trailhead

FEE Free

TREAT YOURSELF Grab a burger from the Honey Island General Store, which was established more than 80 years ago at the intersection of FM 1293 and FM 1003.

Big Thicket National Preserve, Hickory Creek Savannah Unit
(409) 951-6700
Facebook @BigThicketNPS

plant. A carnivorous plant, it eats meat (bugs)! This trail includes a short inner loop (0.3 miles) and a longer outer loop (1 mile). Today you'll be hiking the outer loop, which shares its final stretch with the inner loop. From the trailhead, take the trail on the right to begin the outer loop counterclockwise. You'll pass a wooden bridge and soon hit the first of several boardwalk stretches along the hike. As you hike through the pine savannah—grassy plains with a few trees—keep your eyes open for the sundews: dime-sized red flowers peeking up alongside the boardwalk. Near the end of the hike the trail will split; this is where the outer loop meets the inner loop. This intersection marks the best place to spot sundews, which typically bloom in late spring and early summer. From here both forks take you back to the trailhead. The trail on the left passes through a savannah with abundant summer wildflowers, and the trail on the right passes by a bog that is home to pitcher plants.

SCAVENGER HUNT

Longleaf pine

Young longleaf pines look like something out of a Dr. Seuss book, sort of like a pom-pom on a stick. Forests of longleaf pine used to cover much of the coastal plains of the southeastern states from Texas to Virginia. Today, only 3% of their forests remain, due to logging, development, and fire suppression. Longleaf pine restoration

is a huge priority for Big Thicket National Preserve. It's possible to pick out the longleaf pines from the others due to their larger cones and their much-longer needles. As you hike, gather a few of the long needles and see if you can weave them together for a bracelet. Native Americans made intricate baskets from these. The trees also are pyrophytic, meaning that they are fire-resistant, which can help them outcompete other plants.

Pinus palustris has long needles and very large cones

Pink sundew

The sticky droplets on the end of their leaves give these plants their name, sundew. Did you know there are meat-eating plants? The sundew is one example, and Big Thicket has four out of the five species that exist in North America! Don't worry—they are not dangerous to humans or other mammals. The plants consume small insects only. Sticky hair on the leaves attract and trap the prey, then they coil in on top of it. You can find sundew in areas with plenty of flies and lots of moisture. Play sundew tag and stay in place while the "flies" around you try to get past!

The Big Thicket contains four species of carnivorous plants; this is *Drosera capillaris*

Pitcher plant

Pitcher plants capture their prey by luring insects toward them with color, nectar, and scent. The pitcher of the flower is coated in a slippery, waxy substance. Once an insect lands on it, it slides down the funnel into the inner part of the plant, which digests the insect protein. Only the exoskeleton of the insect remains. Can you imagine what an insect skeleton looks like? Pick an insect and draw it in your nature journal.

The open funnel of *Sarracenia alata* waits to capture an insect

American sweetgum

A sweetgum tree can be easily recognized by its five-pointed, star-shaped leaves. These are bright green in spring and summer and turn yellow, orange, or red in fall. It blooms with pale green flowers in early spring and drops lots of ball-shaped seedpods after. If you find a pod, feel how spiky it is!

Liquidambar styraciflua; Spiky sweetgum seedpods

ADVENTURES IN
THE COASTAL PLAINS

The Coastal Plains are the wettest region of Texas, with hot, humid summers and mild winters. The area offers sandy beaches on the Gulf Coast's barrier islands, alligator sightings in the marshes, and birdwatching galore. The Rio Grande Valley is perhaps the best birding hot spot in North America, with many species appearing here at the northernmost part of their range. You'll also find the Great Texas Coastal Birding Trail, a network of 43 trails with observation decks, boardwalks, and more. Begin in the Houston area, where you'll climb to the top of a 60-foot observation deck, birdwatch from a gazebo on the Brazos River, traverse alligator territory, and watch fireflies. Then you'll hop on Highway 59 and head southwest to one of the last remaining stands of South Texas brush country at Lake Corpus Christi State Park. A short jaunt southeast along I-37 takes you to Padre Island National Seashore for a beach hike. Then it's time to head to the border of Mexico! You'll take Highway 77 toward I-69 East and Harlingen to explore two World Birding Center sites, Resaca de la Palma State Park to the east and Estero Llano Grande State Park to the west. Grab your binoculars and let's get started!

43

CLIMB THE TOWER AT SHELDON LAKE STATE PARK

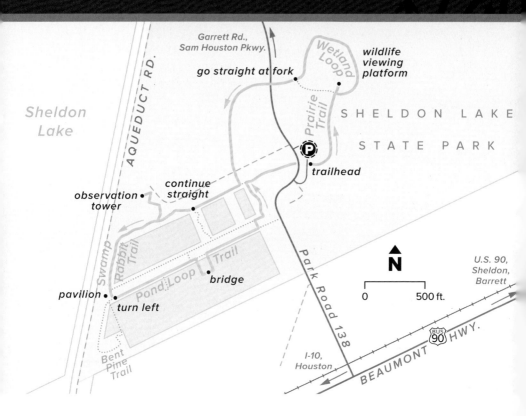

Sheldon Lake

Garrett Rd., Sam Houston Pkwy.

go straight at fork

Wetland Loop

wildlife viewing platform

SHELDON LAKE

STATE PARK

AQUEDUCT RD.

Prairie Trail

trailhead

continue straight

observation tower

Swamp Trail

Rabbit Trail

Pond Loop Trail

bridge

pavilion

turn left

Bent Pine Trail

Park Road 138

N

0   500 ft.

U.S. 90, Sheldon, Barrett

I-10, Houston

BEAUMONT HWY.

BUS 90

YOUR ADVENTURE

Adventurers, today you'll be hiking through an oasis of plant and animal species on the outskirts of the biggest city in Texas. This coastal prairie land is the historical homeland of the Akokisa and was once filled with towering bald cypress trees, shallow wetlands, and tall grasses. When European settlers arrived, much of this land was converted into private farms and

The view of the boardwalk from the top of the observation tower →

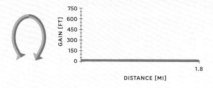

GAIN [FT]

750
600
450
300
150
0

1.8

DISTANCE [MI]

LENGTH 1.8-mile loop

ELEVATION GAIN 6 ft.

HIKE + EXPLORE 1 hour

DIFFICULTY Easy—except for the climb to the top of the tower, all level

SEASON Year-round.

GET THERE The park is located on the northeast side of Houston. Heading northbound on Beltway 8, exit at Garrett Road. Turn right at the stoplight. (If you're heading southbound on Beltway 8, take the Garrett Road exit and turn left.) After you turn, follow Garrett Road for 2 miles. You'll see Park Road 138 and the entrance on your right. From the entrance, continue 1.9 miles to the Prairie Trail parking lot and trailhead.

GOOGLE MAPS: bit.ly/timbersheldon

RESTROOMS Between the Pond Center and Aquatic Lab 1

FEE Free

TREAT YOURSELF Enjoy some boba tea at Bibo's Cafe, 7 miles south of the park on Beltway 8.

Sheldon Lake State Park & Environmental Learning Center
(281) 456-2800
Facebook @SheldonLakeStatePark

ranches. Currently, a restoration project is underway to restore and preserve the prairie. You'll start your hike where the parking lot meets the Prairie Trail and turn right, away from the reservoir. This part of the trail boasts a beautiful boardwalk leading up to a wildlife-viewing station. After exploring here, you'll take a short additional loop to your right, called the Wetland Loop. When it merges back with the Prairie Trail, continue straight. After a road crossing, you'll complete the final stretch of the Prairie Trail loop before crossing a boardwalk. After that, turn right onto the Swamp Rabbit Trail to head toward the observation tower—stay straight past several other trails until you reach the tower. Climb the stairs more than 82 feet in the air, taking time to enjoy scenic views of the prairie and the Houston skyline in the distance. After the tower, you'll continue on the Swamp Rabbit Trail where the boardwalk begins until you turn left to join the Pond Loop Trail. Before you reach the end of your hike you'll pass a bench and come across a bridge leading to a pond overlook on your right. Alligators live here, so be careful. You may also spot turtles, frogs, or a variety of aquatic birds. When you're done here, you're ready to hike back on the Pond Loop Trail for the final stretch back to the trailhead.

SCAVENGER HUNT

American alligator

These reptiles are not picky eaters. They prefer meat but will eat fruits and vegetables as well. Alligators are not interested in humans because we are too big and fast to make good prey. An alligator will very rarely chase a human on dry land, but if they do, they

won't go far. Still, it's a good idea to give them at least 30 feet of space. Can you measure that out to see how far back you should stay from an alligator?

Please heed the warning signs; *Alligator mississippiensis* can weigh up to 1000 pounds!

John Jacob Observation Tower

When you climb to the top of the tower, you'll see Sheldon Lake and view restored prairieland. If you look closely, you can also see some buildings in the distance. This is the downtown Houston skyline. Can you spot it? The tower is named for Houstonian John Jacob—what would you like named after you?

Ascend over 82 feet when you climb to the top of the tower

Hoof fungus

Hoof fungus is also called tinder fungus because it has been used as tinder to start fires for thousands of years. First you remove the hard outer portion, then save thin strips of the inner, spongy layer to use as tinder. Have you ever started a campfire? How did you do it?

Fomes fomentarius is shaped like a horse's hoof

Eastern pondhawk

These insects come in a few different colors. Adult males are powdery blue with a yellow-tipped abdomen. Adult females are bright green with dark spots on the abdomen. Young males are green like females but change colors as they

get older. These dragonflies like warmth, so you may find them resting in the sunshine. Do you usually prefer to hang out in the sun or shade?

Erythemis simplicicollis is a dragonfly that lives in ponds and still waters

44

WATCH FOR BIRDS AT EL FRANCO LEE PARK

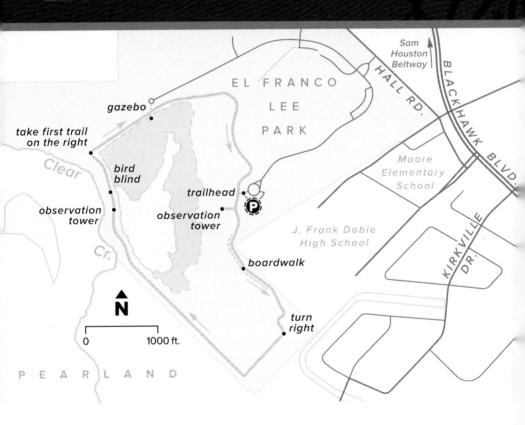

EL FRANCO

LEE

PARK

Sam
Houston
Beltway

HALL RD.

BLACKHAWK BLVD.

gazebo

take first trail
on the right

Clear

bird
blind

trailhead

observation
tower

observation
tower

Moore
Elementary
School

J. Frank Dobie
High School

KIRKVILLE DR.

boardwalk

Cr.

N

0   1000 ft.

turn
right

P E A R L A N D

YOUR ADVENTURE

Adventurers, today you'll be hiking through an urban park in the largest city in Texas, which sits on the historical homelands of the Akokisa. From the trailhead, go left to hike clockwise around the park. You'll quickly come upon an observation tower. Climb to the top and look for birds and other wildlife. After the tower you'll reach the boardwalk. The trail will

The boardwalk at El Franco Lee Park →

GAIN [FT]

750
600
450
300
150
0

2.1

DISTANCE [MI]

LENGTH 2.1-mile loop

ELEVATION GAIN 16 ft.

HIKE + EXPLORE 1 hour

DIFFICULTY Easy—Short and flat

SEASON Year-round.

GET THERE From central Houston, take the Gulf Freeway Frontage Road southeast and turn right (south) onto Blackhawk Boulevard. Turn left on Southbluff Boulevard and then take an immediate right onto Hall Road. When you enter the park, continue 0.6 miles past the ball fields to the last parking lot in the line, where you'll find the trailhead.

Google Maps: bit.ly/timberelfrancolee

RESTROOMS At the nearby El Franco Lee Community Center

FEE Free

TREAT YOURSELF Grab a donut from Dobie Donuts, right by the park on Blackhawk Boulevard.

El Franco Lee Park
(346) 286-1805
Facebook @CommissionerPrecinctOne

soon make two right turns to stay within the park's boundaries. The path straightens out for about 0.5 miles before arriving at another observation tower and a bird blind wall. Soon, you'll turn right and head to a gazebo. You're nearing the end of your hike now, but this is a great place to stop and enjoy a snack break with a view of the water as you look for wildlife. Return to the trailhead to complete the loop. Check out El Franco Lee's playground and splash pad. For a bigger Houston adventure visit the Houston Museum of Natural Science—just 20 minutes away—which is home to a planetarium, a rainforest conservatory with a 50-foot waterfall, and a butterfly center.

SCAVENGER HUNT

Alligator flag

Alligators often hide among these water plants. Look closely for multiple purple flowers in spring. When you see the leaves shaking, that means an alligator is moving around close by. Do you see any leaves shaking today?

Thalia geniculata (means "bent" in Latin) carries its large, lance-shaped leaves on long stalks

Killdeer

Look for these birds walking or running along the ground. They usually run for a few steps, stop to look around, and then continue on their way. If they feel a threat or disturbance on the ground, they will fly into the air and circle overhead while making repeated calls. They can be pretty noisy, which is how they got their scientific name. If you had to pick a scientific name for yourself, which of your characteristics would you want it to describe?

Charadrius vociferus (means "loud" in Latin)

Gazebo

Be sure to stop at the gazebo for some wildlife observation. The park is home to many species of birds that can be grouped into three categories: residents, at the park year-round; migrants, during spring and fall when they pass through; winter visitors, during the colder months before returning north for summer. If you can identify a bird in the park, ask a grown-up to help you find out in which category it belongs.

A gazebo for wildlife observation toward the end of the trail

Monarch butterfly

Monarch butterflies migrate through here twice a year, from their breeding grounds in the north to their overwintering areas in Mexico. During fall and spring, you'll find them passing through Texas on their way from one place to another. Although they travel long distances, monarchs are picky eaters. They only eat a wildflower called milkweed. If you had to eat one food your whole life, what would it be?

You may find *Danaus plexippus* at the butterfly garden in fall and spring

Green anole lizard

These reptiles are usually a bright green color, but they can change to brown or gray depending on their mood and the temperature. What does your body do when you change moods? They usually turn from green to brownish-gray when they are feeling threatened or cold. These lizards are diurnal, meaning they are active in the daytime like us. They spend their time hunting spiders, flies, crickets, ants, and other prey or basking in the sun. Does eating and relaxing in the sun sound like a good day to you?

Anolis carolinensis is a tree-dwelling lizard that can change colors

45

BE ALLIGATOR ALERT ON THE 40 ACRE LAKE TRAIL

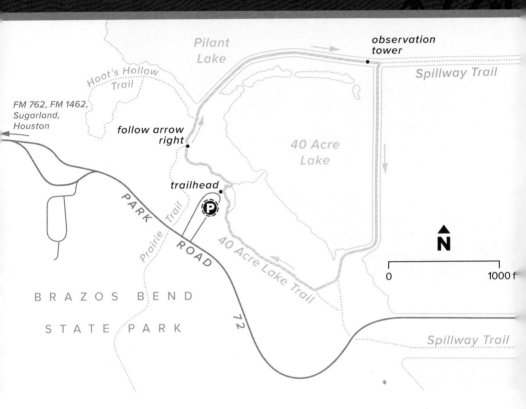

Pilant Lake

observation tower

Hoot's Hollow Trail

Spillway Trail

FM 762, FM 1462, Sugarland, Houston

follow arrow right

40 Acre Lake

trailhead

PARK ROAD

Prairie Trail

40 Acre Lake Trail

BRAZOS BEND

STATE PARK

72

N

0   1000 f

Spillway Trail

YOUR ADVENTURE

Adventurers, today you'll venture into alligator territory as you explore
several aquatic habitats on the historical homeland of the Capoque band
of the Karankawa. From the 40 Acre Lake Trail restrooms take a left for a
clockwise hike around the lake. Before you reach the lake, notice that the
trail slopes downward. This is the ancient bank of the Brazos River, which

A winter view of the 40 Acre Lake →

GAIN [FT]

750
600
450
300
150
0

1.2

DISTANCE [MI]

LENGTH 1.2-mile loop

ELEVATION GAIN 26 ft.

HIKE + EXPLORE 1 hour

DIFFICULTY Easy—Short and level, good for all skill levels; be sure to stay out of the water, as this is alligator territory, and stay at least 30 feet away from any that you see— slowly back up if you find yourself any closer.

SEASON Year-round. Alligator nesting season is June to early September.

GET THERE The park is about an hour drive from downtown Houston. Take Highway 288 south to FM 1462 West. Follow FM 1462 West to FM 762 North. The park entrance is on the right. The parking lot and trailhead are just after the park headquarters.

Google Maps: bit.ly/timber40acre

RESTROOMS At the parking lot

FEE $7 for adults; free for children 12 and under; free with Texas State Parks annual pass

TREAT YOURSELF Enjoy a slice of pie from The Jay Cafe, 18 miles west in Needville.

Brazos Bend State Park
(979) 553-5101
Facebook @BrazosBendStatePark

is now located several miles away. You'll walk past open marshes before you reach the observation tower. When you get there, climb to the top to view the lakes, marshes, and swamps that are home to more than 300 bird species. When you climb back down, stay right on the 40 Acre Lake Trail, passing the Spillway Trail, until you reach the trailhead. For an evening stargazing adventure, check out George Observatory, open Saturday nights at the park (advance tickets required) or spend the night at a Brazos Bend campsite.

SCAVENGER HUNT

Alligator hatchlings

Look for snouts poking out of the lake water as you walk. Mother alligators build nests on the bank, lay their eggs (30 to 50 of them!), then guard them until they are ready to hatch. Baby alligators are tiny—about 6 to 8 inches long—and stay with their mothers for up to two years. The females can get very defensive when they have a nest or hatchlings. Never approach any alligator, especially not a mother with her young or a nest! Did you know a group of baby alligators is called a "pod"?

Alligator nesting season is from June to early September

Great egret

This bird was nearly wiped out in the United States during the late 1800s because its plumes (feathers) became such popular fashion items. Eventually, conservationists helped put measures in place to protect the bird colonies, and egrets made a comeback. These majestic birds have a wingspan of 50 to 55 inches. How big is that compared to your arm span? What about your other family members?

Ardea alba is a tall, long-legged bird with an S-curved neck

Southern live oak

Some of the live oak trees in the park are so old that they were seedlings when this area was still claimed by Spain in the 1700s. These oaks have technically lived in Spain, Mexico, the Republic of Texas, the United States, the Confederacy, and then the United States again—some of them have been in five different countries without moving an inch! What is another country that you would like to visit one day?

Quercus virginiana is a stately tree with a wide canopy and horizontally arching branches

40 Acre Lake

From the top of the observation tower, you're surrounded by three unique aquatic ecosystems. You'll be able to see a lake, a marsh, and a swamp. Can you tell which is which? A marsh is like a shallow lake with soft-stemmed plants growing most of the way across it, like a flooded prairie. A

swamp is like a flooded forest. It has to have two things—trees and water—at least part of the year. And a lake has to have some area where the water is deep enough that sunlight can't penetrate to the bottom. Sometimes an aquatic ecosystem is a mixture of all three. Which do you like best?

Can you tell the difference between a lake, a marsh, and a swamp?

46

HIKE TO THE BANKS OF THE BRAZOS RIVER

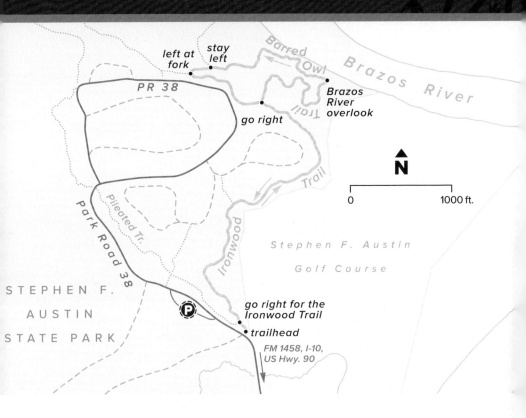

YOUR ADVENTURE

Adventurers, today you'll hike to the banks of the Brazos River, close to the site of an old ferry crossing near the historic town of San Felipe de Austin. Established by Stephen F. Austin on remote, Mexican-owned land, the town was once the unofficial capital of the European colonies. This area is also the historical homeland of the Karankawa. In 1823, Stephen F.

A winter hike through the woods of Stephen F. Austin State Park →

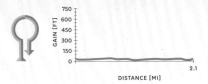

LENGTH 2.1-mile lollipop

ELEVATION GAIN 46 ft.

HIKE + EXPLORE 1 hour

DIFFICULTY Easy—A flat hike through the woods

SEASON Year-round. Late spring to early summer is a great time to see wildflowers and wildlife. White-tailed deer fawns are born as early as April and as late as July.

GET THERE From Houston, travel west on I-10. Take Exit 723 (San Felipe/Frydek) to FM 1458 (just before Sealy). Turn right (north) and take FM 1458 for 2 miles, then turn left onto Park Road 38. Proceed 0.8 miles to the entrance. From the park entrance, take the next left for the parking lot. The trailhead is across the street.

Google Maps: bit.ly/timberstephenfaustin

RESTROOMS At the headquarters and in a building close to the trail 0.5 miles into the hike

FEE $5 for adults; free for children 12 and under; free with Texas State Parks annual pass

TREAT YOURSELF Enjoy some tamales or friend ice cream at Mesquite Mexican Grill, 5 miles southwest of the park, in Sealy.

Stephen F. Austin State Park
(979) 885-3613
Facebook @StephenFAustinStatePark

Austin—often called the "Father of Texas"—brought nearly 300 settler families to live here under a contract with the Mexican government called an "empresario." Over time, the colonists grew discontented with the Mexican government. They declared their independence during the Texas Revolution, which they won in a battle nearby in 1836. Your hike to the river will be considerably more peaceful today. Start at the Ironwood Trail, heading right. You'll cross a metal bridge and continue until it meets up with the Barred Owl Trail. (Shortly before this merge, you'll pass restrooms—there are none at the trailhead so you may want to use these.) At the Barred Owl Trail, turn right to head to the banks of the Brazos River. As you continue on the trail you'll see several forks to the right with additional river overlooks. Stay left to continue your hike along the Barred Owl Trail, then stay straight as you pass the Sycamore Trail. Eventually you'll take a big left to merge back onto the Ironwood Trail and return to the trailhead.

SCAVENGER HUNT

Osage orange

Named after the Osage people, this tree's wood was a favorite for making bows. This is how it gets its other name—*bois d'arc* (French for "wooden bow") tree. It was also used as a pre-barbed wire fence by early colonial farmers. They'd plant the trees close together and the arching, thorny branches would create a prickly barrier. It was also among the first batch of plant samples sent back to England by the Lewis and Clark Expedition in the early 1800s. During World War I, a dye made from the roots and bark was widely used to produce khaki-colored military uniforms for the United States Army. Have you ever used dye made from a plant in your artwork or other projects?

Maclura pomifera

Brazos River overlook

The Brazos River is the eleventh-longest river in the United States and one of the largest rivers in Texas. It's sometimes used to unofficially mark the boundary between East and West Texas. The river begins in the plains northwest of Dallas/Fort Worth, flows through that metropolitan area past

College Station, and empties into the Gulf of Mexico. Can you think of any reasons why rivers were historically important for building cities?

This trail takes you to the banks of the 840-mile-long Brazos River

Black vulture

Black vultures have a black head and only the tips of the wingspan are white. These birds usually roost in large groups on the bare branches of dead trees. Because they eat the carcasses of dead animals (called "carrion"), they are associated with death, but these birds are important for the living. They play a huge role in eliminating possible sources of disease spread by dead animals, which helps keep other animals, including humans, healthier. What do you think of vultures—cute, creepy, or crafty cleaners?

Coragyps atratus (means "darkened" in Latin)

Fireflies

When an animal, plant, or other organism in nature produces light, it's called bioluminescence. Bioluminescence involves producing a glow that emits lots of light but very little heat. When fireflies light up, nearly all of the energy goes to produce light. By comparison, a light bulb is 90% heat and only 10% light. When you get home, turn on a light bulb and carefully feel it after a few minutes. Do your bulbs at home produce heat?

In May and June, fireflies put on a light show at dusk

47

CRUISE TO LAKE CORPUS CHRISTI

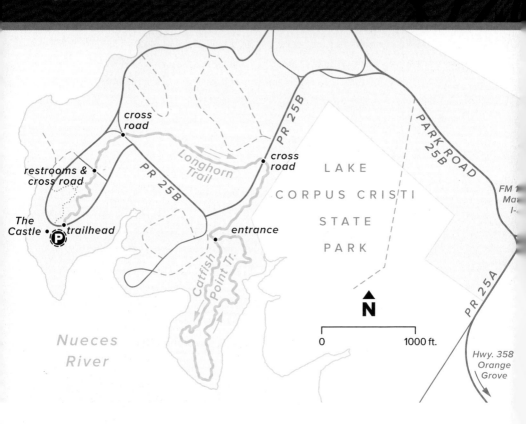

YOUR ADVENTURE

Adventurers, imagine that you're a colorful bird that spends summers in Canada and winters in South America. You make one-way trips of up to 10,000 miles. When your journeys are that long, you need a comfortable place to land along the way, and Lake Corpus Christi State Park provides exactly that for many birds. The state park is located on the historical

Lake Corpus Christi →

GAIN [FT]

750
600
450
300
150
0

2.5

DISTANCE [MI]

LENGTH 2.5-mile lollipop

ELEVATION GAIN 75 ft.

HIKE + EXPLORE 1.5 hours

DIFFICULTY Easy—Level, with a loop around the lake

SEASON Year-round. Spring brings beautiful blooms, butterflies, and migrant birds.

GET THERE From Mathis, take FM 1068 to Highway 25. The park entrance is 0.5 miles down the road on the left. From the park entrance, follow the signs for the Old Pavilion (also known as "The Castle"). The parking lot is used for both The Castle and the Longhorn Trail.

Google Maps: bit.ly/timbercastle

RESTROOMS About 5 minutes into the hike, along the Longhorn Trail

FEE $5 for adults; free for children 12 and under; free with Texas State Parks annual pass. Be sure to reserve a day-use pass in advance, especially during peak seasons.

TREAT YOURSELF Kona Ice offers shaved ice treats at the park on weekends and some weekdays.

Lake Corpus Christi State Park
(361) 547-2635
Facebook @LakeCorpusChristiStatePark
Instagram @lakecorpuschristi

homelands of the Karankawa and Lipan Apache. You'll begin your hike today on the Longhorn Trail—you can find the trailhead near the Old Pavilion ("The Castle"). A short way into the hike you'll reach a set of restrooms, then cross a small park road. After the road, continue on the Longhorn Trail until you reach another road crossing. Stay on the Longhorn Trail, keeping an eye out for the trail marker. After a longer stretch you'll come across a final road crossing and remain on the Longhorn Trail on the other side. Follow a wooded path until you reach the trailhead for the Catfish Point Trail. It's a loop—you can go either clockwise or counterclockwise. This section of the trail boasts beautiful views of Lake Corpus Christi. When you emerge from the Catfish Point Trail, take the Longhorn Trail back to The Castle. When you're done hiking, spend the rest of the day enjoying the open waters of the lake. For an added adventure, snag a campsite and spend the night.

SCAVENGER HUNT

The Castle

This structure was built by the Civilian Conservation Corps (CCC) in the 1930s using caliche, an abundant local rock. It's very similar to limestone but is formed differently. The CCC mixed crushed caliche with cement to create "caliche-crete" blocks. The workers tooled the

surface of those blocks to make them look similar to limestone blocks. By the 1950s, the structure was used as a dance hall. There was a concessions area in the middle surrounded by a dance floor. Can you pretend to go back to the 1950s and do a dance inside this old pavilion?

The old pavilion built by the CCC is called "The Castle" by locals and park staff

Purple sage

Pretty purple sage (also called "cenizo") has signature grayish-green leaves, and its purple flowers bloom generously after summer rain showers. Tea made from purple sage was historically used to treat chills and fevers. Do you ever drink tea when you're feeling sick?

Leucophyllum frutescens (means "shrubby" in Latin)

Neotropic cormorant

The calls of this shorebird have been compared to pig grunts. In Mexico, some people refer to this bird as the pig duck (*pato cerdo* or *pato cuervo*) or the oinking or grumpy duck (*pato gruñon*). Do your best pig-grunt impression as you look for them today.

Nannopterum brasilianum is nearly all black, with a snakelike neck

Anacua tree

The anacua has dark leaves year-round that feel like rough sandpaper. During spring, small white blooms cover the tree, making it look like it's got a light dusting of snow. These flowers are highly fragrant, so when they bloom, the air is wonderfully perfumed. Try to spot one of these trees and feel the leaves. How do they feel compared to other leaves?

Ehretia anacua is a medium-sized tree found in southern Texas and eastern Mexico

48

MALAQUITE BEACH WALK

Malaquite
Campground

Corpus Christi

wooden
overlook

PADRE

ISLAND

NATIONAL

SEASHORE

PARK ROAD 22

Visitor
Center

trailhead

Gulf
of
Mexico

N

0   2000 ft.

boundary
markers

YOUR ADVENTURE

Adventurers, today you'll be exploring Malaquite Beach on the historical homelands of the Malaquite. Malaquite Beach makes up a small section of Padre Island, where it is one of the only sections protected from vehicle traffic. This makes it a great place to hike, swim, run, and play. Park at the Malaquite Visitor Center and take a short boardwalk down to the beach.

Malaquite Beach is on the Gulf side of Padre Island →

LENGTH 2.4 miles out and back

ELEVATION GAIN none

HIKE + EXPLORE 2 hours

DIFFICULTY Easy—A placid walk on the beach

SEASON Year-round.

GET THERE From Corpus Christi, head east on Highway 358. After crossing the JFK Causeway onto Padre Island, Highway 358 changes to Park Road 22. Continue south 10 miles on Park Road 22 to reach the park entrance, then continue another 5 miles to the visitor center.

Google Maps: bit.ly/timbermalaquite

RESTROOMS Yes

FEE $10 per vehicle

TREAT YOURSELF Head back up to Corpus Christi to enjoy a shaved ice treat at Sno Ball or Sno Ball Too.

Padre Island National Seashore
(361) 949-8068
Facebook @PadreIslandNPS

The visitor center is located between Malaquite Campground (0.5 miles north) and the southern boundary of the car-free area (0.5 miles south). Start your hike by heading left toward Malaquite Campground. In 0.5 miles you'll see a wooden boardwalk and overlook that takes you to the campground. If you hop up onto the overlook, you'll see a sign listing many of the seashore's bird species. Nearly 400 species have been found at Padre Island National Seashore. How many can you spot? Hike back a mile until you hit the southern boundary of the beach, marked by a series of wooden poles. Here, turn around and head back toward the visitor center. After the hike, take a dip in the ocean and enjoy a picnic on one of the beach's several picnic tables.

SCAVENGER HUNT

Atlantic ghost crab

This small crustacean (animal with an exoskeleton) is a sand-colored crab with white claws. Sometimes larger than 2 inches across, they can dig burrows in the sand up to 4 feet deep to seek shelter from the hot sun! Its eyes give it 360-degree vision, which helps it spot and catch insects for food. They do not know how to swim, although female crabs can float upside down in the water. Its strong legs help it run up to 10 miles per hour, or about 15 feet in one second. How long does it take you to run 15 feet?

Boo! *Ocypode quadrata*

Greater moon jelly

This cnidarian (an invertebrate animal with tentacles that can sting) blends in with the sand from a distance, but up close you can easily see their cool, jellylike texture. Among the least dangerous jellyfish to humans, there is no need to worry if you run into or accidentally step on one. But not touching them is smart. If they don't look like a fish, that's because they aren't. Many marine biologists prefer the term "jelly" instead of "jellyfish" to avoid confusion. How many differences between fish and jellyfish can you think of?

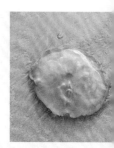

Aurelia labiata

Brown pelican

In coastal areas you can find brown pelicans flying single file in groups over the water. They have big wingspans, up to 6 feet across. Their diet consists almost entirely of fish. Watch them swoop out of the air to catch a meal. They dive headfirst from as high as 60 feet in the air, plunge into the water, and usually emerge with a fish in their bill. Do you think the fish see them coming?

Pelecanus occidentalis

Sea turtle hatchlings

These sea turtles are critically endangered, but marine biologists at Padre Island National Seashore are working to help them. After taking up to four days to hatch in area nests, the baby turtles are released—typically from the middle of June until the end of August. Members of the public can gather at dawn to watch them crawl toward the ocean. Newly hatched sea turtles are about the size of a small cookie. How big were you when you were born?

The hatchling release of *Lepidochelys kempii* is a special summer event!

49

ROAM THE RESACA

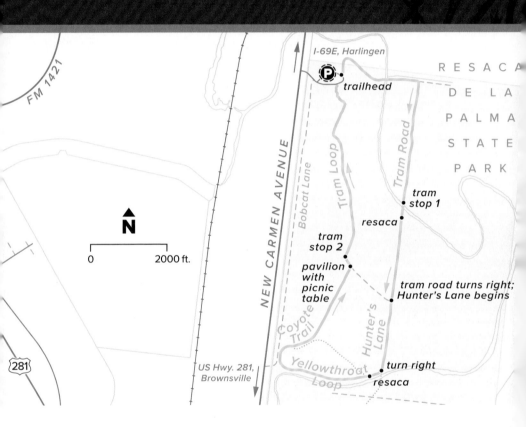

Resaca de la Palma has 8 miles of trails and a tram loop running through the park →

YOUR ADVENTURE

Adventurers, today you'll be hiking on the historical homelands of the Coahuiltecan. The land is also part of the 1200 semitropical acres that make up the World Birding Center, so bring your binoculars! If you want to hike the whole trail, walk along the Tram Loop to Tram Stop 1, passing the Mesquite Trail and the Mexican Olive Trail. If you catch the tram, hop

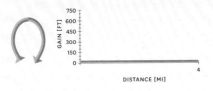

GAIN [FT]

750
600
450
300
150
0

DISTANCE [MI]

4

LENGTH 4-mile (or 2-mile) loop

ELEVATION GAIN 36 ft.

HIKE + EXPLORE 2 hours without the tram; 1 hour with the tram.

DIFFICULTY Challenging if you take the full hiking trail and return on the Tram Road (4 miles); easy if you ride the tram to Stop 1 and hike to Stop 2 (2 miles). Tours of the park travel by free electric tram a few times a day. The ride is staffed by knowledgeable and friendly volunteers or park rangers. The tram follows a 2.75-mile loop around the park, making a few stops along the way. You can hop on for the tram loop then check out separate hiking trails on foot. Call the park before your hike to get the schedule.

SEASON Spring and fall migration seasons are wonderful times to see many types of birds.

GET THERE From Route 77/83, exit at Olmito. Follow FM 1732 west for 2.5 miles, then turn left and follow New Carmen Avenue to the visitor center and main parking lot.

Google Maps: bit.ly/timberresaca

RESTROOMS At the headquarters

FEE $4 for adults; free for children 12 and under; free with Texas State Parks annual pass. Be sure to reserve a day-use pass in advance, especially during peak seasons.

TREAT YOURSELF The State Park Store at the headquarters offers a good selection of cold beverages, snacks, and ice cream.

Resaca de la Palma State Park
(956) 350-2920
Facebook @resacadelapalma

off at Tram Stop 1, which is right at the Second Bridge. There is a resaca (former riverbed) crossing here, a great spot for sighting colorful birds like the ringed kingfisher and Altamira oriole. Go straight along the Tram Loop until it runs into the Hunter's Lane trailhead. Hike down Hunter's Lane until you reach another resaca crossing. Look for more bird species like the white-faced ibis and roseate spoonbill. Without crossing the resaca, turn right to head toward the Yellowthroat Loop. When the trail forks, stay left for the edge of the loop closer to the water. After some time you'll reach Bobcat Lane—turn right here to stay on the Yellowthroat Trail. Soon, turn left to join Coyote Trail, which will take you to a mesquite woodland, past a pond, then bring you to Tram Stop 2. If the tram is running, hop on and ride it back to the visitor center. If not, there is a covered picnic table down the road where you can power up before you hike the final 1.5 miles back along the tram loop.

SCAVENGER HUNT

Resaca
The park periodically controls the water level, flooding the resaca, which creates a habitat that supports a large variety of wildlife, including nearly 300 species of birds. When the resaca is dry, not many birds will be around. Why do you think the birds prefer water?

A resaca is a dry riverbed

Buff-bellied hummingbird
This hummingbird has a red bill with a black tip, rust-colored tail feathers, and iridescent green throat. While most hummingbirds fly south for winter, this one flies north to Louisiana. Bird scientists (ornithologists) don't know why. Why do you think they do it?

Amazilia yucatanensis likes to sip nectar from flowers

Gulf Coast toad

The backs of these amphibians vary in color from olive green to nearly black, but they all have a light tan underbelly. Toads usually rest in cool, sheltered spots during the day. At dusk, they come out to feed on insects. You can also hear them "singing" most nights from March to September. Have you heard them before?

Incilius nebulifer measures 2 to 4 inches long

Ringed kingfisher

These birds are not very tall, but their wingspan can reach up to 2 feet. They have strong wings and can fly for long stretches of time. They like to fly high in the air, following rivers or streams below. To catch prey, they will often perch on branches, waiting for the perfect moment to swoop down. They eat fish, reptiles, crustaceans, and occasionally even smaller birds. When they are done, they sometimes cough up a pellet of bones and other inedible parts of their prey. Maybe you can find pellets on the ground today. If you were a scientist studying birds, what would you like to find out?

Megaceryle torquata is a large and noisy bird

Texas lantana

This plant loves hot, dry spots where other plants may struggle. It produces bright, pretty, multihued flowers that attract butterflies and hummingbirds. Gardeners love it because it doesn't require much water. How do you look when you need a drink of water?

Colorful *Lantana urticoides* blooms from spring to first frost

50

BIRDWATCH AT THE RIO GRANDE VALLEY

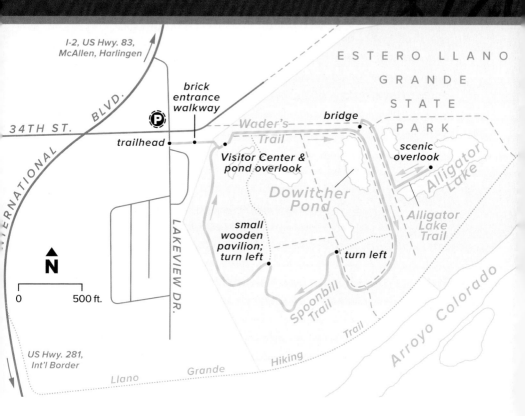

I-2, US Hwy. 83,
McAllen, Harlingen

ESTERO LLANO

GRANDE

STATE

BLVD.

brick
entrance
walkway

bridge

34TH ST.

PARK

Wader's
Trail

trailhead

scenic
overlook

Visitor Center &
pond overlook

Alligator
Lake

Dowitcher
Pond

INTERNATIONAL

LAKEVIEW DR.

small
wooden
pavilion;
turn left

Alligator
Lake
Trail

turn left

N

Spoonbill
Trail

0   500 ft.

Arroyo Colorado

US Hwy. 281,
Int'l Border

Hiking

Llano   Grande   Trail

YOUR ADVENTURE

Adventurers, today you'll hear nature's symphony as you hike in the 230 acres
that make up the largest wetland environment in the World Birding Center
network. These are the historical homelands of the Coahuiltecan. No cars
are allowed past the parking lot, so you'll be able to hear birdsong, frog calls,
and the hum of buzzing insects. To start, find the Entrance Walkway just past

The Entrance Walkway from the parking lot to the visitor center and pond overlook →

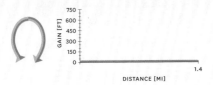

GAIN [FT]
750
600
450
300
150
0

1.4

DISTANCE [MI]

LENGTH 1.4-mile loop

ELEVATION GAIN 9 ft.

HIKE + EXPLORE 1 hour

DIFFICULTY Easy—A short, flat stroll around the pond

SEASON Year-round.

GET THERE From Route 83, exit at FM 1015/International Boulevard and take FM 1015 south for 2 miles, looking for the brick park entrance sign on the left side of the road. The parking lot is immediately on your right as you enter the park, and the walkway to the visitor center and hike is across the street.

Google Maps: bit.ly/timberestero

RESTROOMS At the visitor center, a short walk from the parking lot

FEE $5 for adults; free for children 12 and under; free with Texas State Parks annual pass. Be sure to reserve a day-use pass in advance, especially during peak seasons.

TREAT YOURSELF Enjoy a cupcake from Happiness Cupcakes, 4 miles northwest of the park park in Weslaco.

Estero Llano Grande State Park
(956) 565-3919
Facebook @EseteroLlano
Instagram @EsteroLlanoGrandeStatePark

the parking lot. Head towards visitor center, where you'll find a beautiful deck overlooking Ibis Pond. From here, take Wader's Trail straight to hike clockwise around the park. After a short stretch along this trail you'll see a bridge on your left, the start of a short out-and-back section of the hike. Cross the bridge and take the Connector Trail to Alligator Lake. Turn left just before the lake to hop on the Alligator Lake Trail to a scenic overlook. There, turn around and head back to the bridge. After crossing the bridge again, turn left to rejoin the Wader's Trail and continue your hike around Dowitcher Pond. Pass the Levee Trail on your left, and when the trail splits, turn left for the Spoonbill Trail. About 0.25 miles later you'll turn left again to rejoin the Wader's Trail for the final stretch around Ibis Pond and back to the Entrance Walkway.

SCAVENGER HUNT

Alligator Lake

Did you know that alligators grow new teeth their entire lives? At any given time, they usually have around 75 teeth in their mouth, but as the teeth break or wear down, they are replaced by new ones. This means alligators may have 3000 teeth or more during their lifetime. How many baby teeth have you lost so far?

This large, deep pond is home to the park's resident American alligators

Black-necked stilt

These birds get their name in part because their long legs look like stilts. They like to stand on one leg as they wade in shallow water in search of food. Do your best black-necked stilt pose. How long can you hold it?

Himantopus mexicanus has long, pink legs and a thick, black bill

Common paraque

Brown, black, and gray plumage camouflages this bird as it sleeps—right on the open ground, in daytime! When dusk comes, they get up and fly around in search of insects to eat. The male birds make interesting sounds, ranging from grunts that sound like frogs to rising whistles.

Nyctidromus albicollis

Roseate spoonbill

These birds get their pink coloring from the foods they eat. They dine on crustaceans such as shrimp and other small aquatic creatures that contain carotenoids, which helps to turn their feathers pink. If you turned the color of the foods you eat, what color would you be?

Platalea ajaja likes to forage in the shallows of both fresh water and salt water

Green jay

You've heard of blue jays, but have you heard of green jays? They are beautiful! Green jays are also among the few bird species known to use tools. They eat insects and may use sticks to pry up loose bark in search of their next meal. What tools do you know of that are good for prying something open?

Cyanocorax (means "blue raven" in Greek) *luxuosus* is noisy and colorful

ACKNOWLEDGMENTS

There is nothing more reaffirming that we live in a world full of caring people than when hard-working rangers, parents, conservationists, biologists, geologists, and hikers call us back or respond to our emails, helping us get that species identification just right or helping us verify the year a major discovery happened on the trail. Special thanks to Lisa Gordon, Alan Crowe, Wanda Olszewski, Le'Ann Pigg, Candyce Johnson, Debbie Hicks, Shaylee Burns, Jason Hairston, Lauren Hartwick, Lisa Fitzsimmons, Jamie Langham, Holly Platz, Lauren Sweat, Madison Haynie, Jessica Deboer, Asa Vermeulen, David Owens, Angelina Fontenot, Todd Spivey, Kate Sherman, Shohn Rodgers, Thomas Milone, Rachel Laca, Boyd Sanders, Jared Shamburger, Joel Janssen, Scott Sharaga, Javier de León, David Heinicke, Josie Gunter, and Delia Metcalf.

Huge thanks to Stacee Lawrence, Cobi Lawson, Mike Dempsey, Matt Burnett, Kathryn Juergens, Melina Hughes, David Deis, Andrew Beckman, Sarah Milhollin, Sarah Crumb, and the entire Timber Press family for believing in another book in this series to help reach Texan families!

And to Wendy's family—to Gail, Xavier, and Jaedon Moore for being my trusty guinea pigs; to my father, Alan, for being an amazing driver and hiker; to my husband, Garrison, for being head GPS tracker and cheerleader and chef; and to my mother, Ginny, for her research skills. This book is about family and having a strong family supporting you makes adventure possible.

To Nina's parents and sister, Ann-Marie, Kim, and Maria: I am lucky to have experienced a childhood of adventure with you.

To her family, Ralph, Elsa, and Linnea: Thank you for being my adventure partners and making this book possible.

To her friends, Sarah, Michael, Pippa, and Cricket: Thank you for joining us and making our hiking trips more fun.

To Wendy, thank you for including me in this wonderful project.

And thank you to all of you for reading this and getting outside with each other! We can't wait to see the adventures you go on.

PHOTO AND ILLUSTRATION CREDITS

All photographs are by the authors with the exception of those listed below.

Carolyn Fannon, Lady Bird Johnson Wildflower Center, p. 199 (top)
Lauren Sweat, p. 155

Alamy
Biosphoto, p. 94 (top)
Bob Gibbons, p. 137 (bottom, inset)
Dianne Leeth, p. 102 (top)

Dreamstime
2day929p. 232 (bottom)
Bill Kennedy, p. 80 (bottom, inset)
Brian Lasenby, p. 232 (top)
Cass Tippit, p. 125 (top)
Cathy Keifer, p. 255 (bottom)
Charles Brutlag, p. 175 (middle), p. 221 (top)
Dan Rieck, p. 153 (top)
Daniel Holmes, p. 102, (bottom)
Daniel Logan, p. 137 (middle)
Dennis Donohue, p. 93 (top)
Ed8563, p. 213 (top)
Ellesi, p. 205 (top)
Gerald Deboer, p. 85 (middle)
Hellmann1, p. 112 (top)
Holly Kuchera, p. 205 (middle), p. 233 (middle)
Irina Opachevsky, p. 77 (bottom)
Iulian Gherghel, p. 161 (top)
Iva Vagnerova, p. 191 (bottom)
Jason Ondreicka, p. 224 (middle)
Jason W. Baker, p. 120

William Wise, p. 113 (top), p. 152 (bottom)
Xbrchx, p. 190

Flickr
©Chase A. Fountain, TPWD; p. 128 (bottom)
John P. Weiser, p. 77 (top, inset)
Mike Ostrowski, p. 165 (xxx)
sonnia hill, p. 89 (bottom, inset)

iStock
Tuzyra, p. 54

Shutterstock
Aleron Val, p. 187 (middle)
Donald Walker, p. 77 (top, inset), p. 103 (middle)
J.J. Gouin, p. 187 (top)
Mariusz S. Jurgielewicz, p. 145 (middle)
MirSiwy, p. 156 (inset)
Nikki Gensert, p. 161 (bottom)
plains-wanderer, p. 76 (bottom)
Thomas Torget, p. 112 (bottom)
YuRi Photolife, p. 183 (top)
Zaruba Ondrej, p. 263 (bottom)

Wikimedia
A. Savin, p. 271 (middle)
Andy Morffew, p. 271 (bottom)
Carlos Abrego, p. 259 (bottom)
©2008 Derek Ramsey (Ram-Man), p. 247 (middle)
Dominic Sherony, p. 271 (top)
Drumguy8800 at English Wikipedia, p. 247 (bottom)
Frank Schulenburg, p. 270 (bottom)
Ianaré Sévi, p. 263 (middle)

Judy Gallagher, 225 (middle)
Larry D. Moore, p. 258
Mokkie, p. 259 (top)
Tony Castro, p. 266 (bottom)
University of Texas at Arlington Libraries Special
    Collections, gift of Virginia Garrett, p. 46
US Fish and Wildlife Service Southeast Region, p. 228 (top)
US Fish and Wildlife Service/Steve Maslowski, p. 141 (top)

INDEX

ABOUT YOUR LEAD ADVENTURERS

BOONE RODRIGUEZ

Wendy holds a master's degree in learning technologies and is a former classroom teacher. As part of her quest to bring science education alive, she worked as a National Geographic Fellow in Australia researching Tasmanian devils, a PolarTREC teacher researcher in archaeology in Alaska, an Earthwatch teacher fellow in the Bahamas and New Orleans, and a GoNorth! teacher explorer studying climate change via dogsled in Finland, Norway, and Sweden. Today, she is a global education consultant who has traveled to more than 50 countries to design programs, build communities, and inspire other educators to do the same. She enjoys mountain biking, rock climbing, kayaking, backpacking, yoga, photography, traveling, writing, and hanging out with her family and nephews. Follow her on social media @50hikeswithkids and email wendy@50hikeswithkids.com.

RALPH BALCK

Nina is a sociologist, university lecturer, and outdoor enthusiast. She spent her childhood in Finland and Michigan before making her way to Texas. Her favorite childhood memories include ice skating on frozen ponds during Finnish winters and taking camping road trips with her extended family across the United States. She now lives in the Austin, Texas area with her husband, two daughters, and an adventure dog. As a family, they believe that a good education means developing a sense of curiosity, wonder, and connection with the world around you and that nature is the perfect place to make this happen. They love to hike, camp, and explore the natural beauty of Texas and beyond. Follow Nina on social media @raisingwildflowerkids and email nina@50hikeswithkids.com.